The Master Works:
Art 2

Copyright Lance Hodge, 2014

ISBN 978-1500166441

Printed in the United States of America

The Master Works:
ART 2

By Lance Hodge

Prologue

If you haven't seen *The Master Works: Art*, 'one', then you've got that to look forward to. Luckily you can enjoy both of these books in whatever order you choose.

In *The Master Works: Art* I told you a little about this art, and an experience I had some time ago with great 'art' that really wasn't. You'll have to catch up and read that if you haven't. There's also some discussion in that first book of the clothing of past President's and some historical perspective regarding the increase in the size of humans in the last couple of hundred years. But, enough of that.

So here we are, the long anticipated *Master Works: Art 2*. In this book we will continue our exploration into 'real' art, the sort of art that looks easy, but of course is not. Sometimes we see great art and say to ourselves "Wow, I could NEVER do something like that", and other times we see great art and say "So what, I could do that". To those of you who see art such as this and think YOU could do it, well, let me tell you, it's easier than it looks, and yes, you *could* do it, *if* you were an artistic genius. Luckily most of us are not artistic geniuses otherwise the world would be so full of great art that nobody would care about it.

So sit back and enjoy. Turn the pages slowly and savor each piece like fine wine, or a nice steak, or the last four Cheetos in the bag; art after all is food for the *soul*.

Lance Hodge

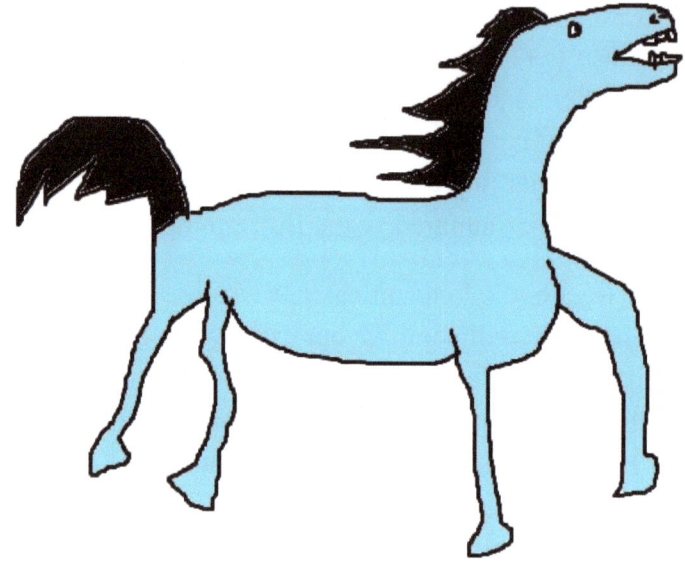

Blue Stallion

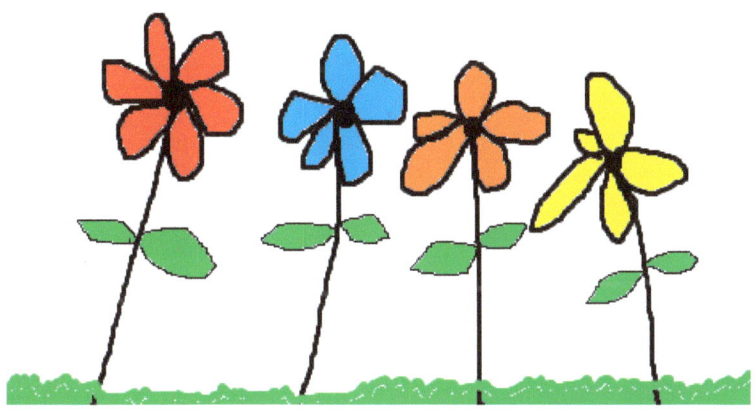

Flowers

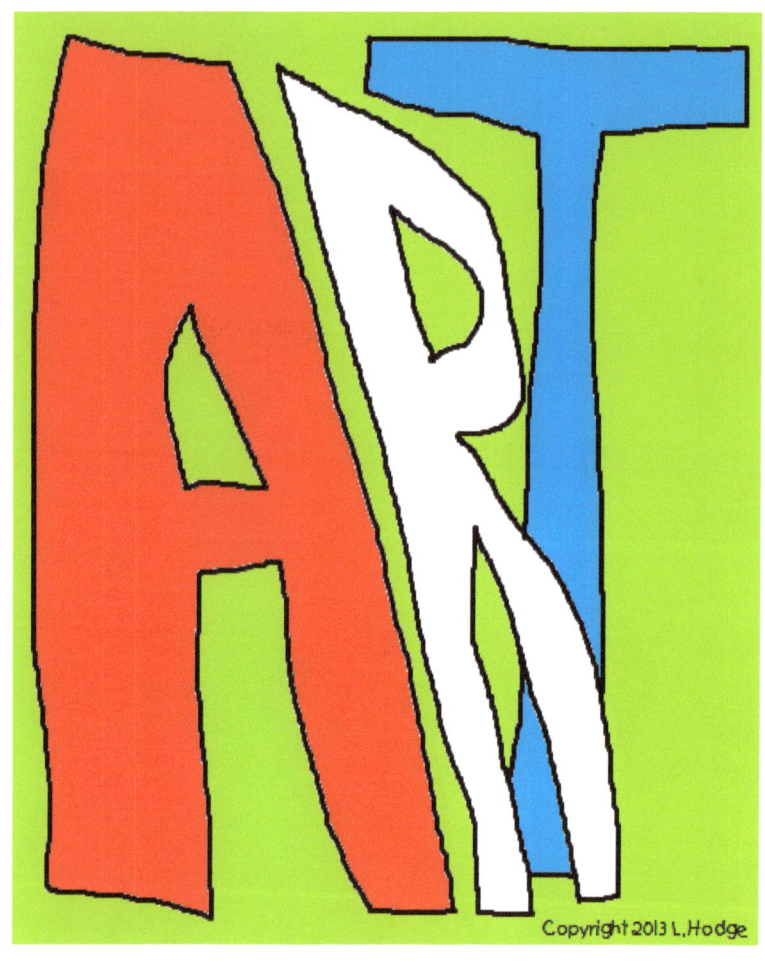

Copyright 2013 L. Hodge

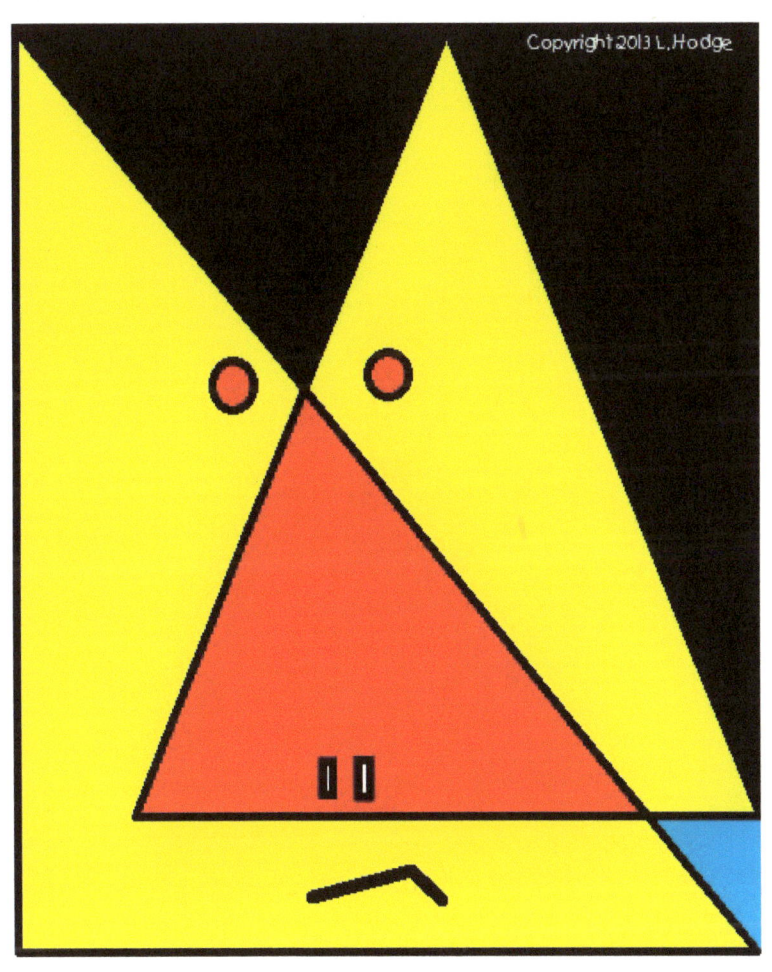

Witchdoctor 2

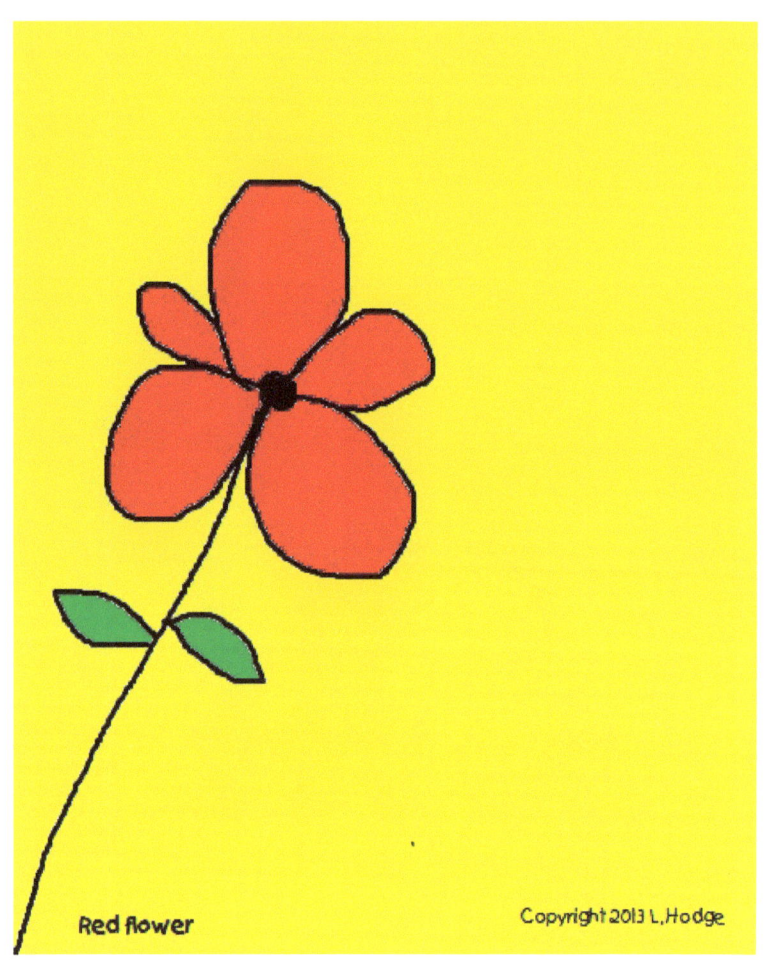

Red flower

Red flower

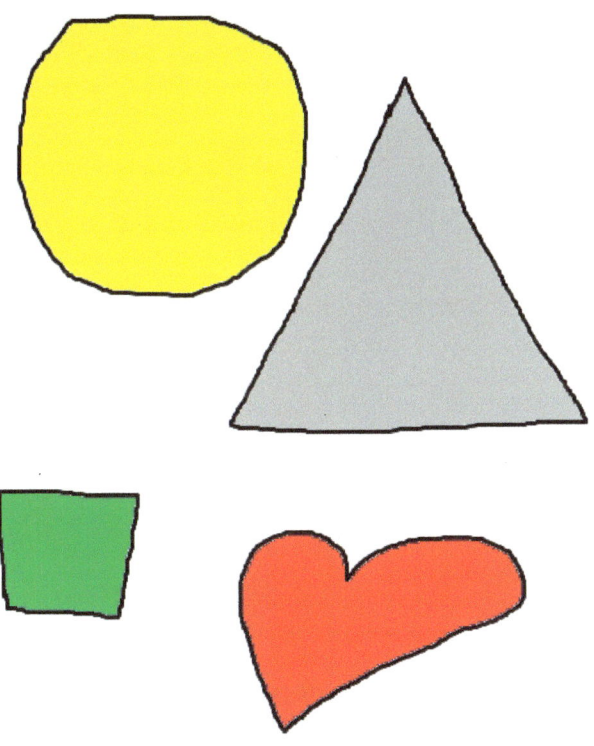

The face of love

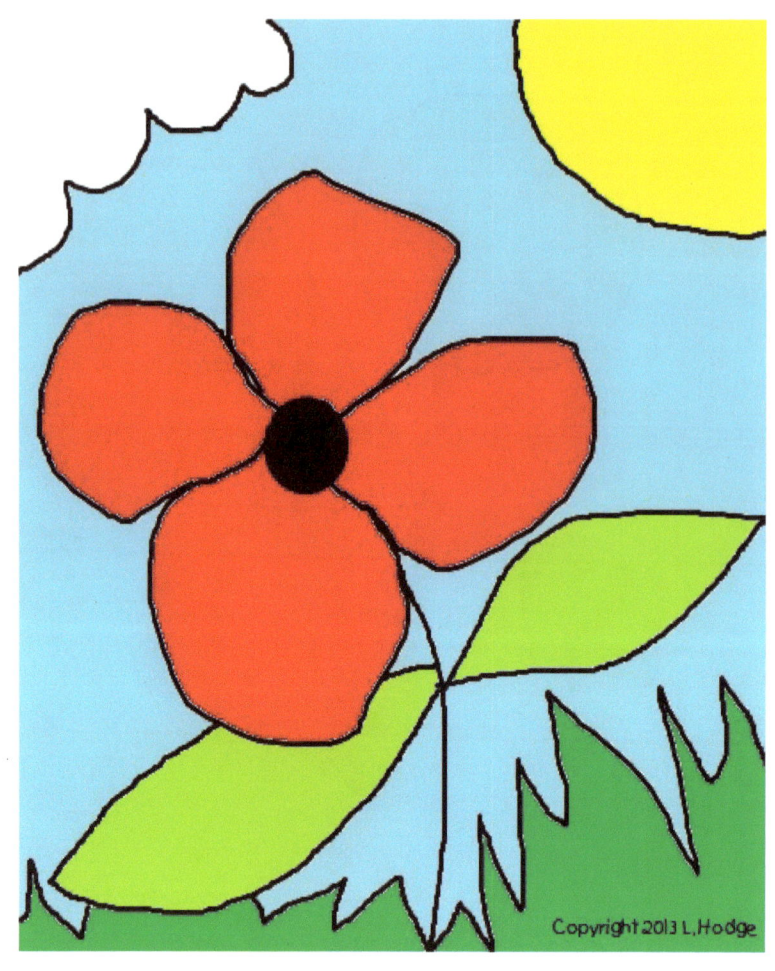

Copyright 2013 L. Hodge

Flower with big leaves

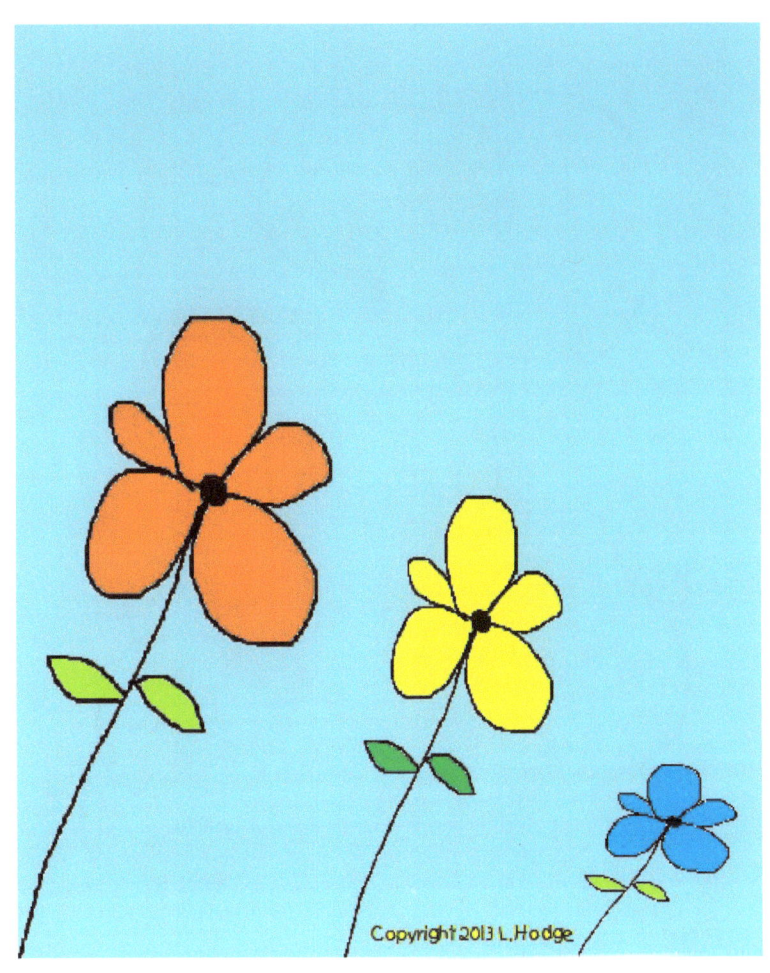

Blue sky

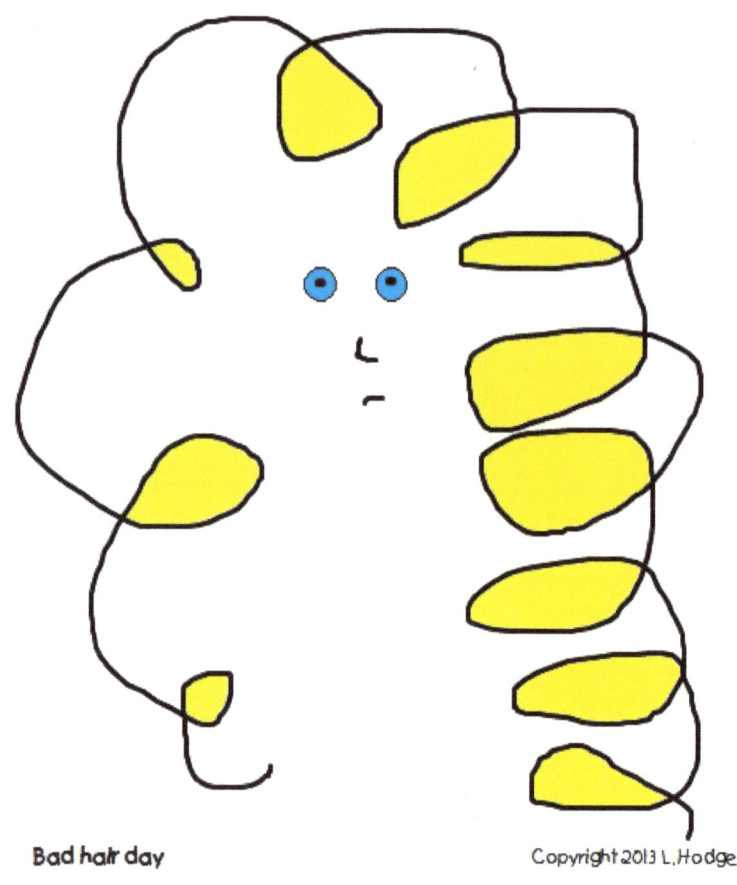

Bad hair day   Copyright 2013 L. Hodge

Bad hair day

Ants heading toward blue flower

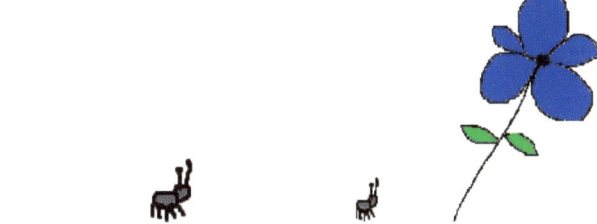

When the 'artist' realizes it's too hard to draw bamboo

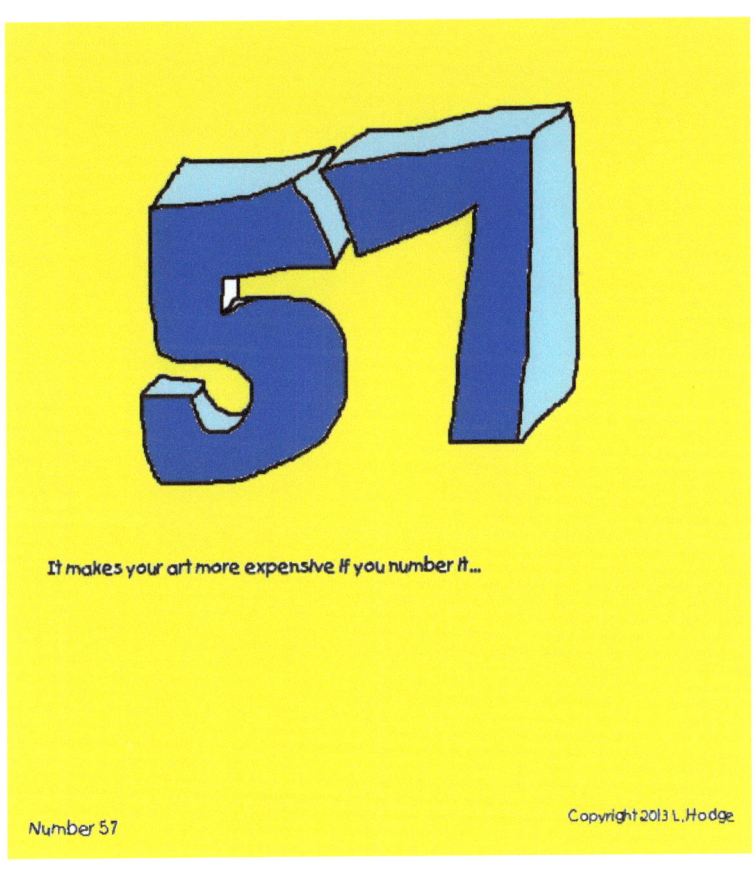

It makes your art more expensive if you number it...

Number 57

57

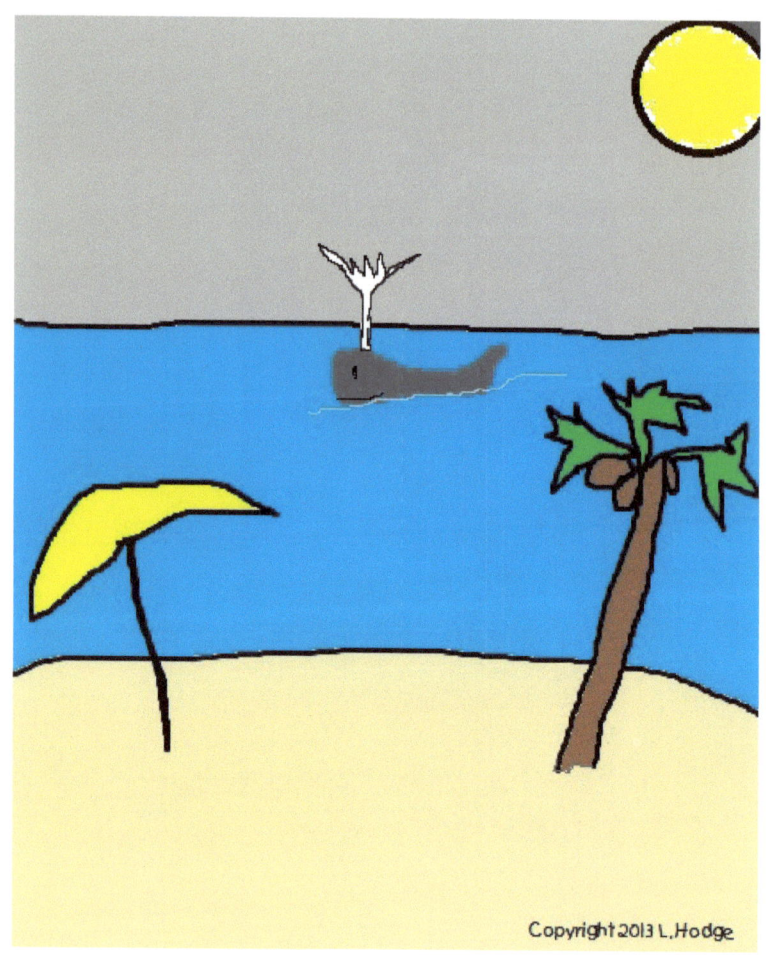

Thar she blows

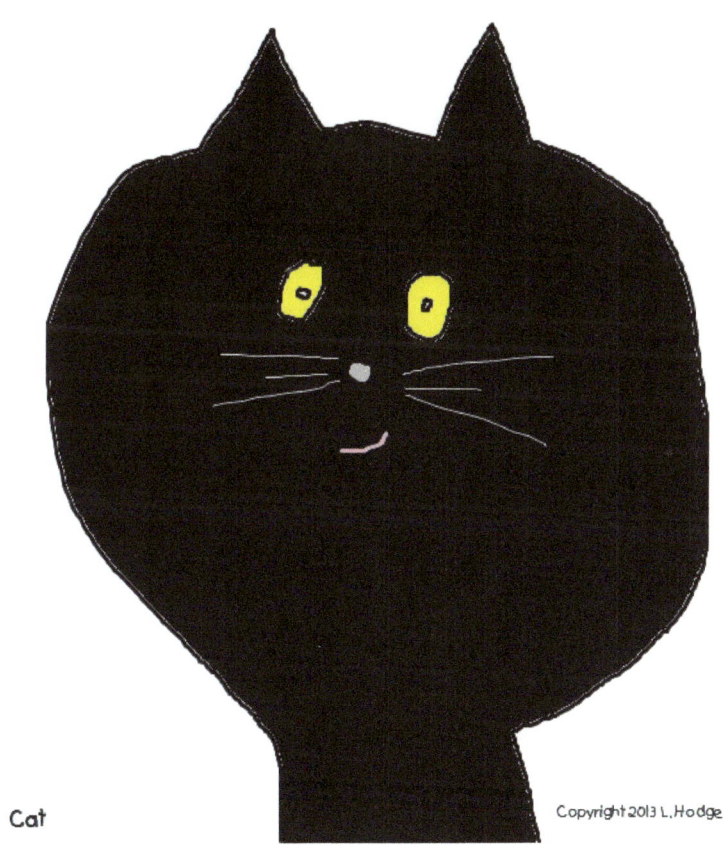

Cat

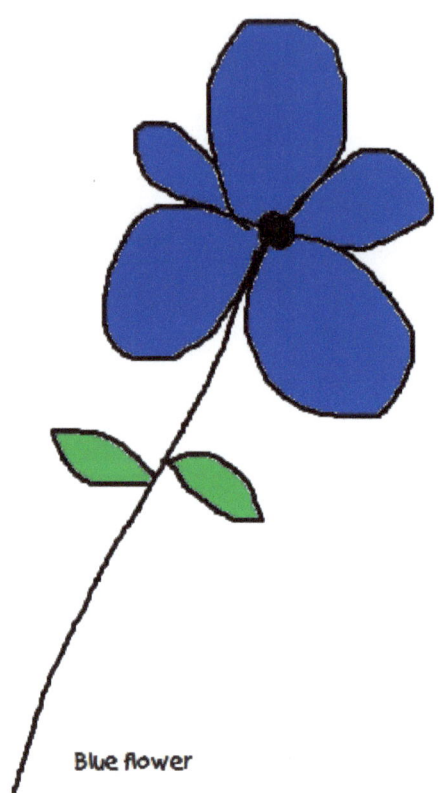

Blue flower

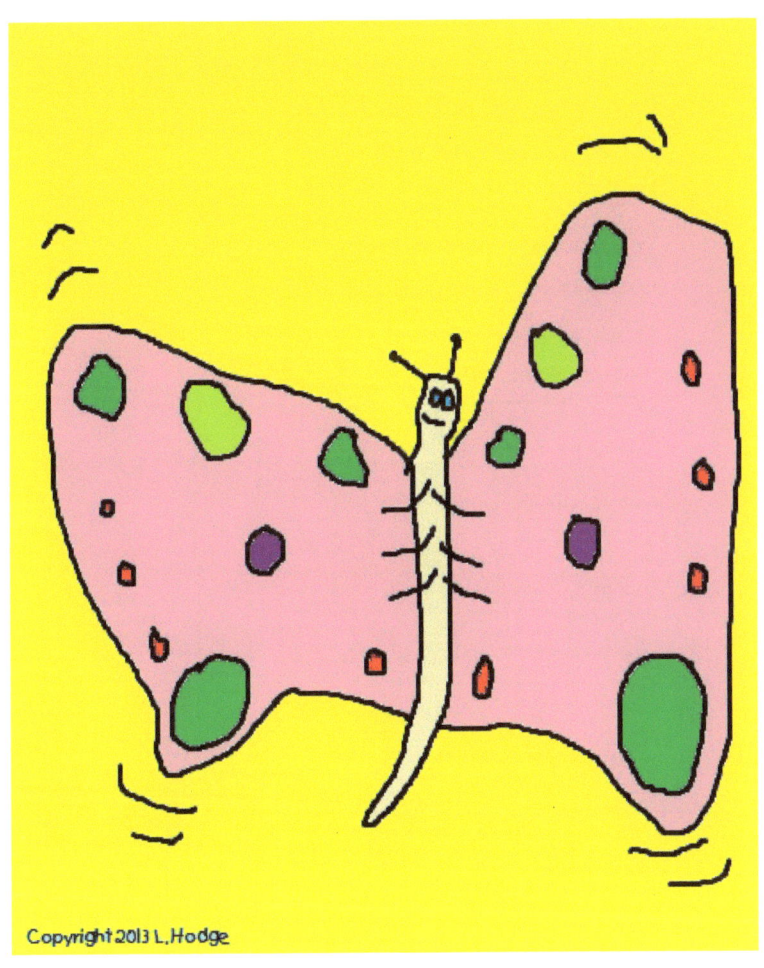

Ex-Caterpillar

19

'Dr. We don't know what to do, he won't stop drawing'

'Just leave him alone, he'll run out of paint'

'He's doing it on the computer'

'Geez'

'How about Haldol?, electro-shock?'

'We could just let him draw, it's not that bad is it?'

'Ok, electro-shock'

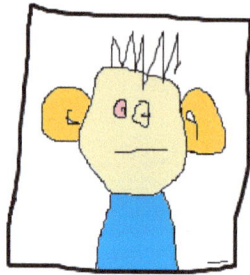 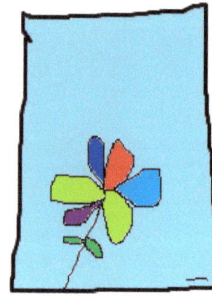 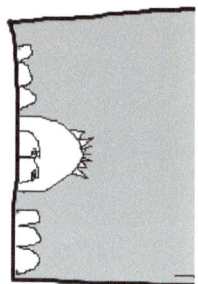

Electro-shock

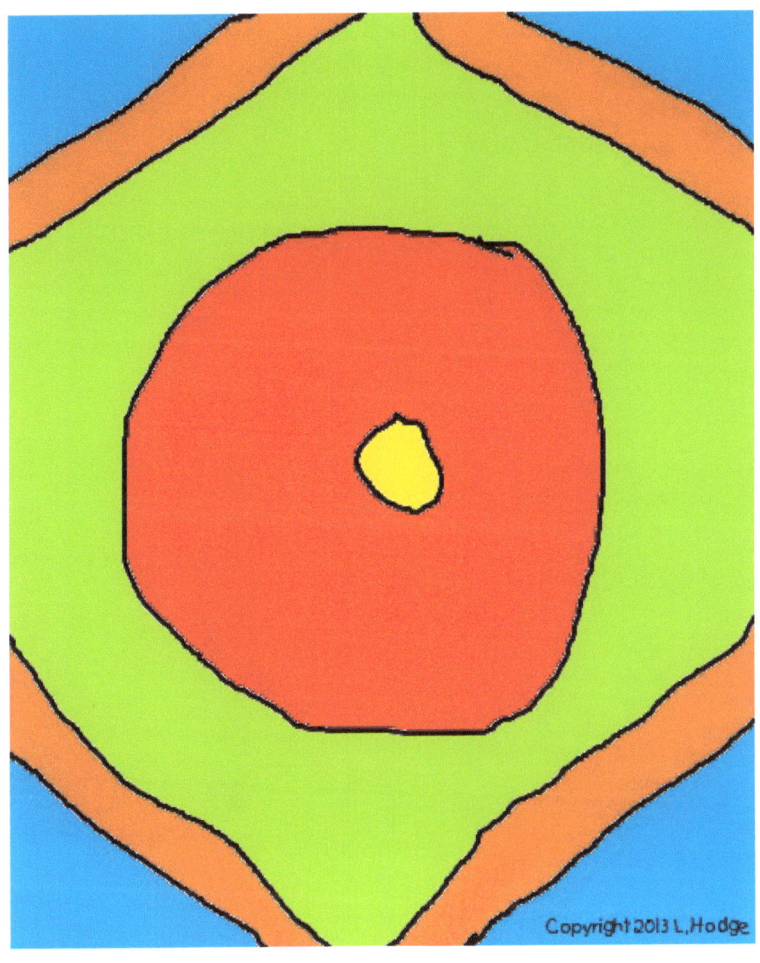

Eye

21

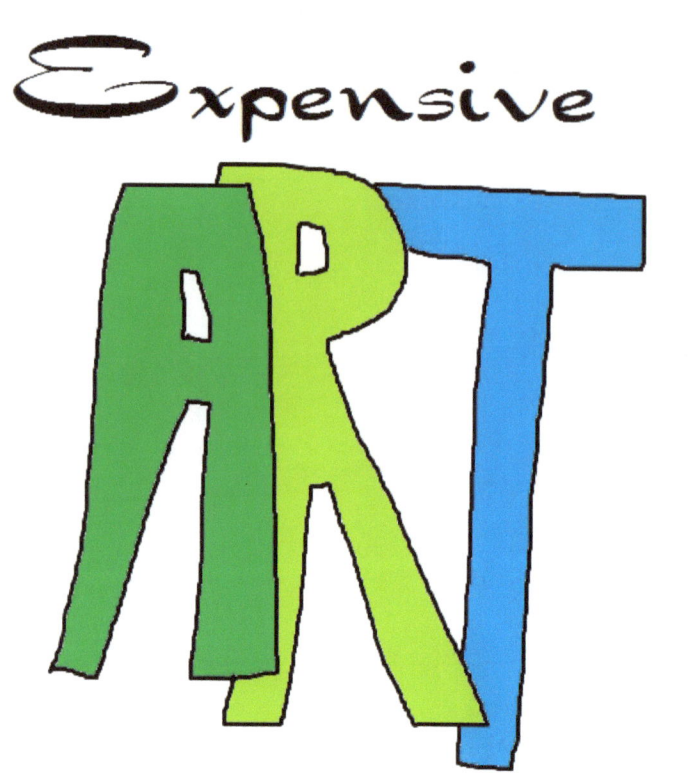

Expensive ART

22

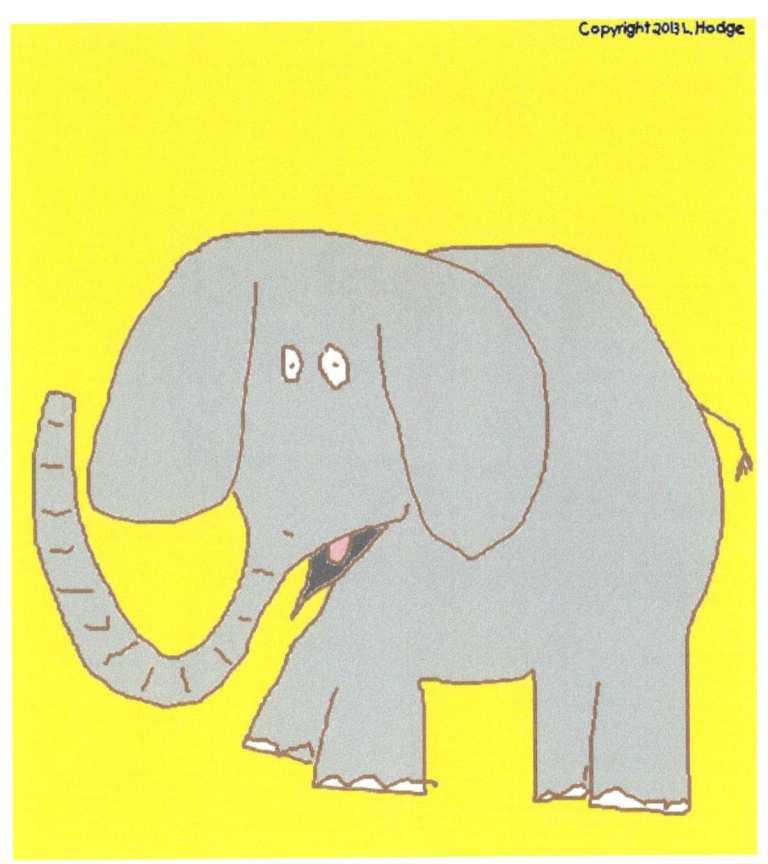

Elephant on yellow

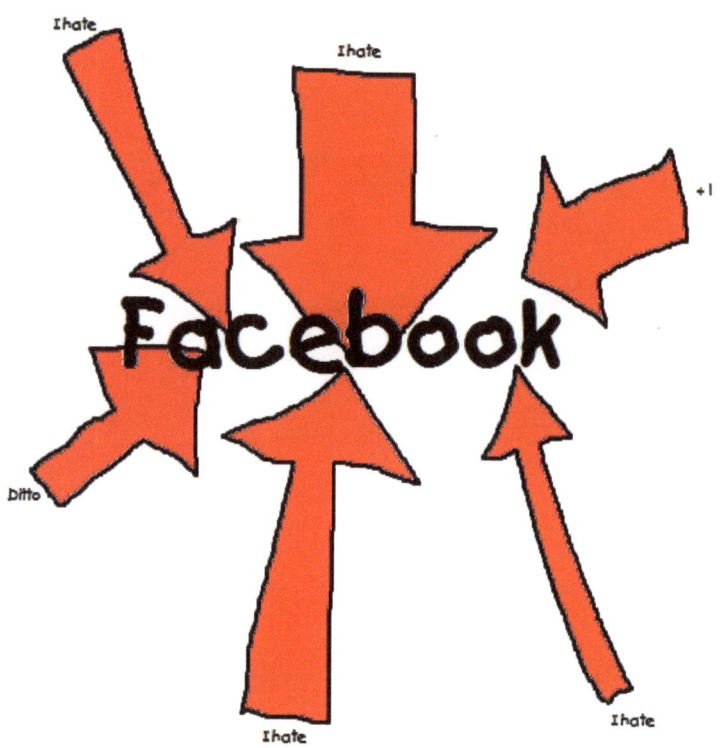

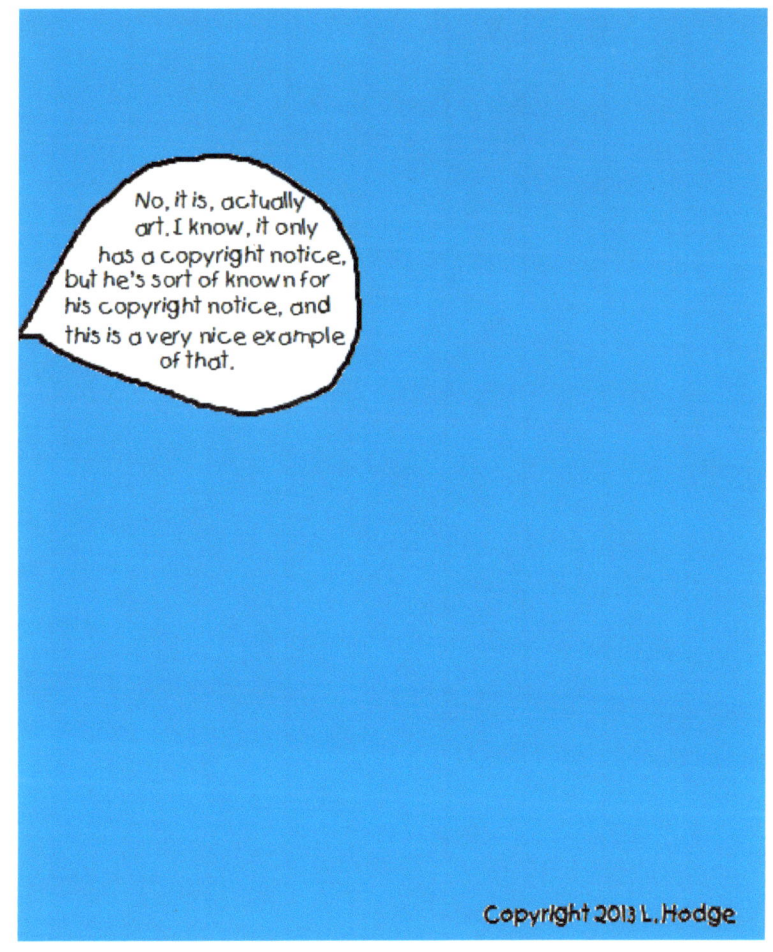

Copyright lost in a snow storm

Cheap

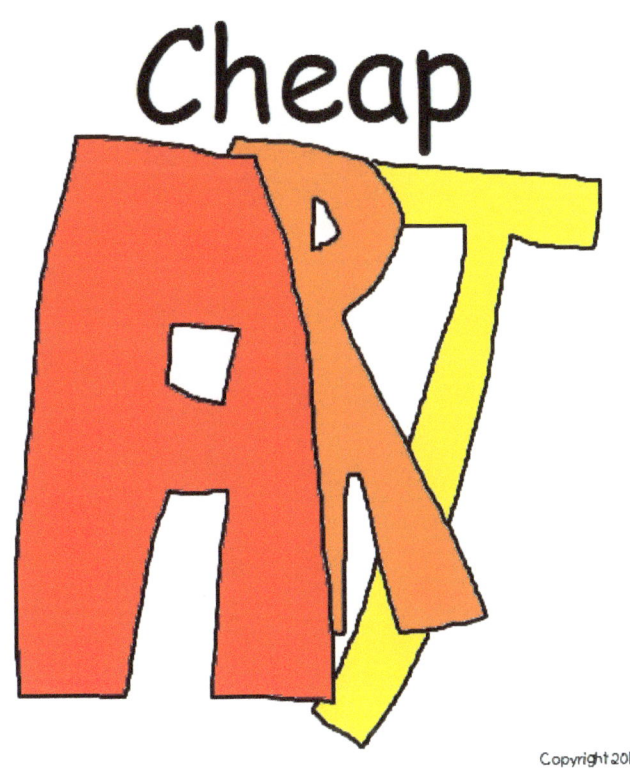

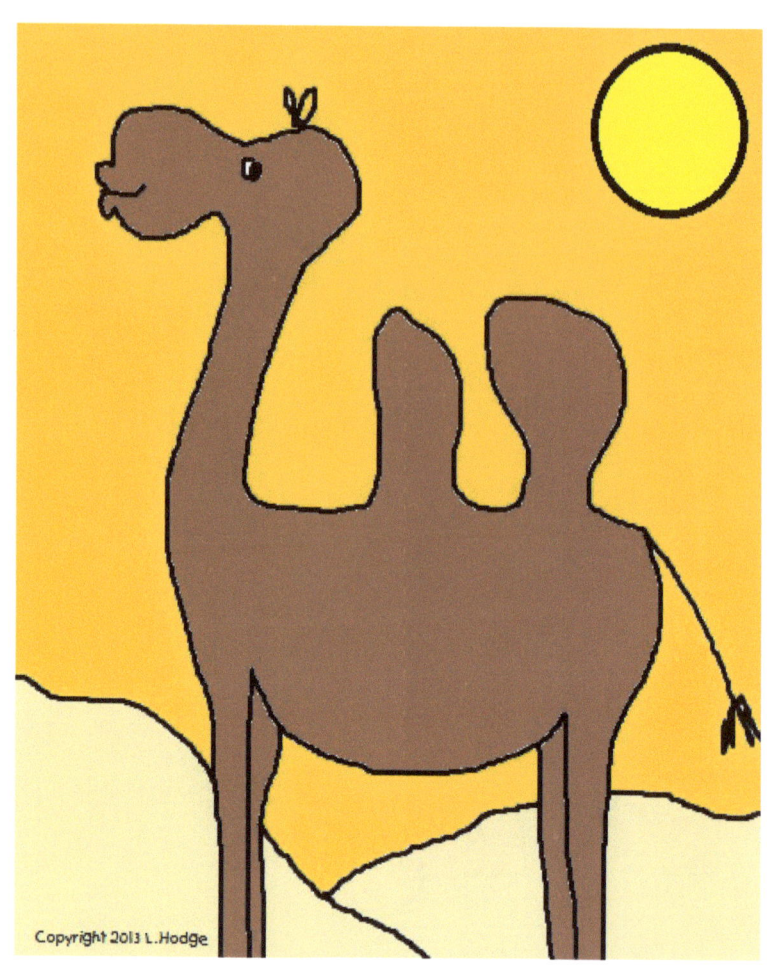

Copyright 2013 L.Hodge

Camel in the sun

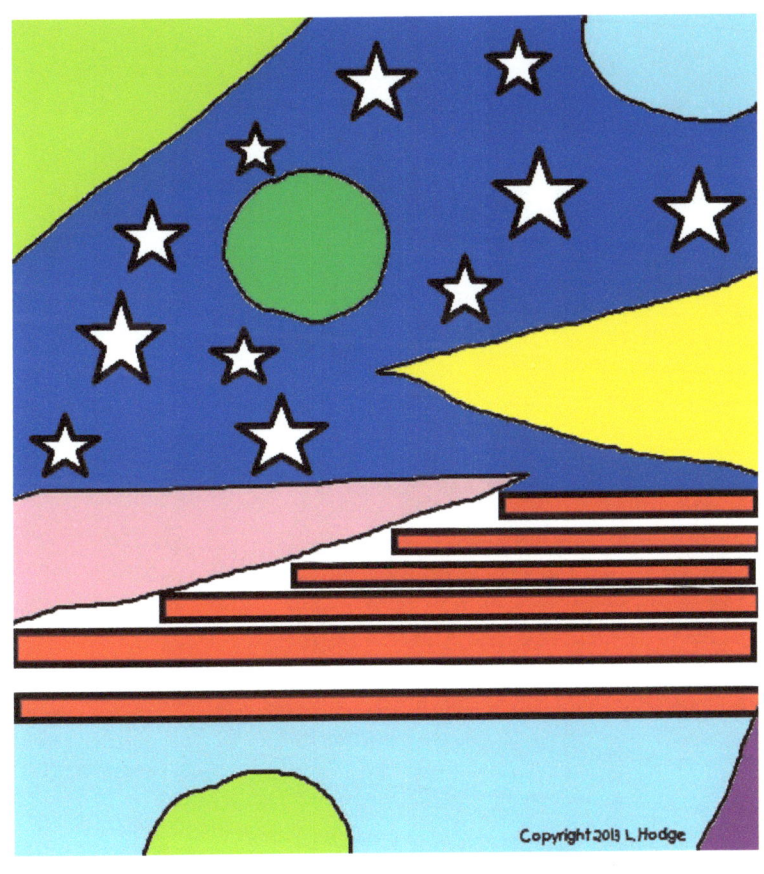

Copyright 2013 L. Hodge

Red, White, and blue... and yellow, and pink, and green, and purple

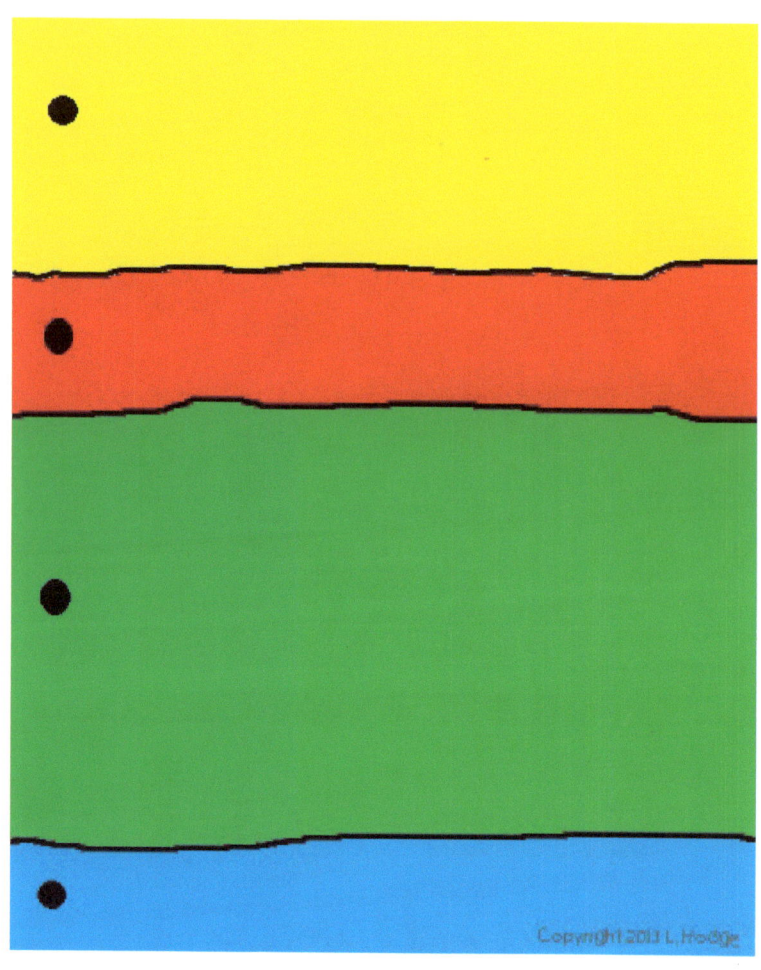

Flag with four grommets

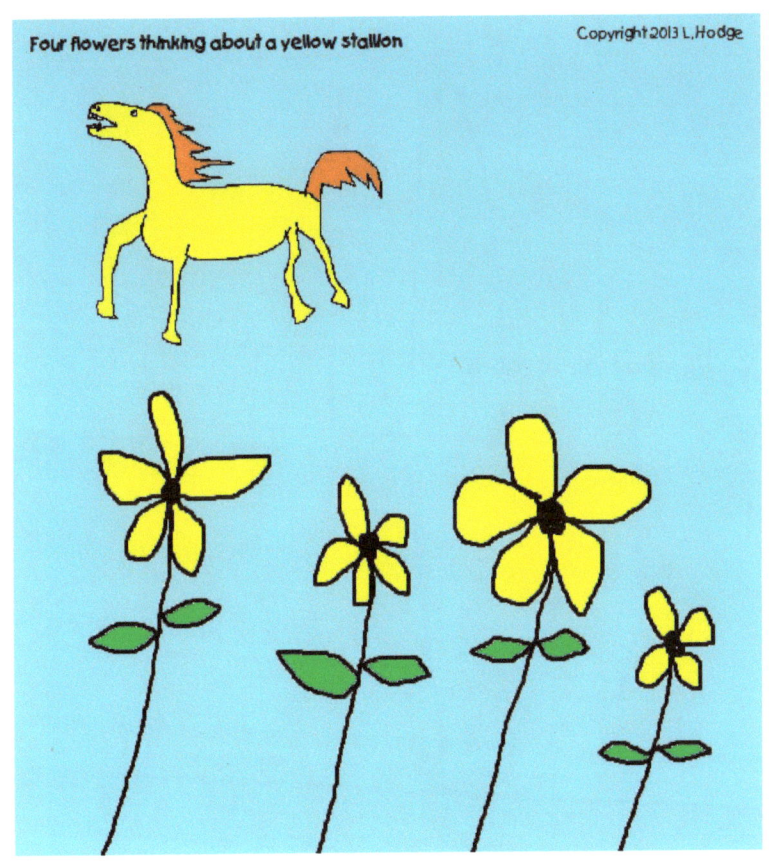

Four flowers thinking about a yellow stallion

Four flowers thinking about a yellow stallion

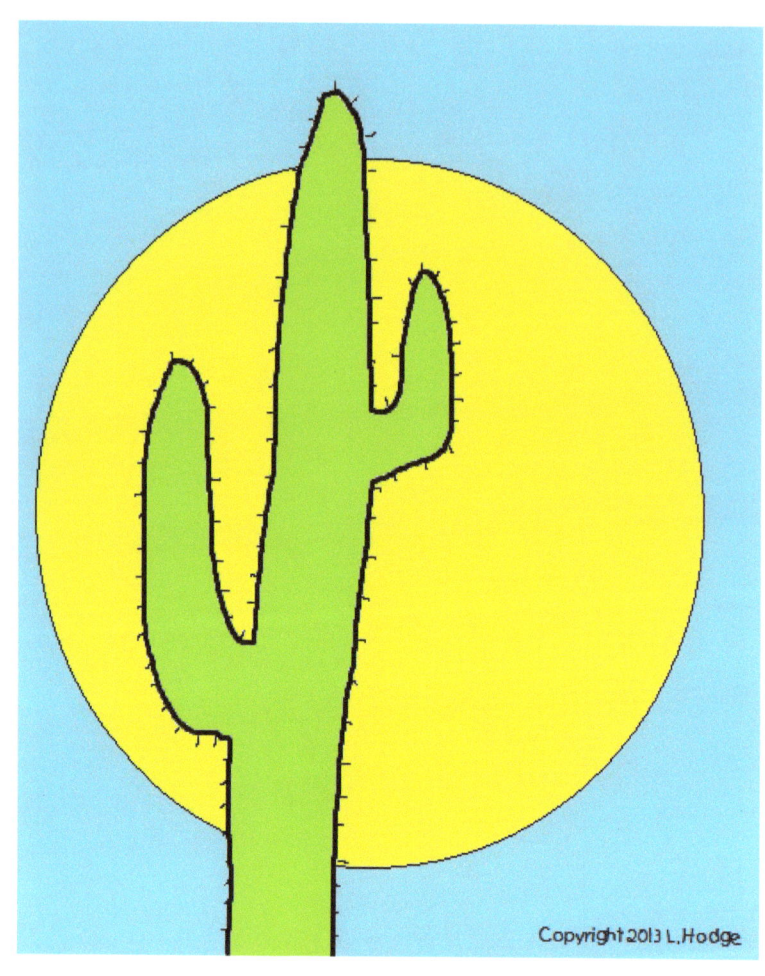

Cactus, sun, and sky

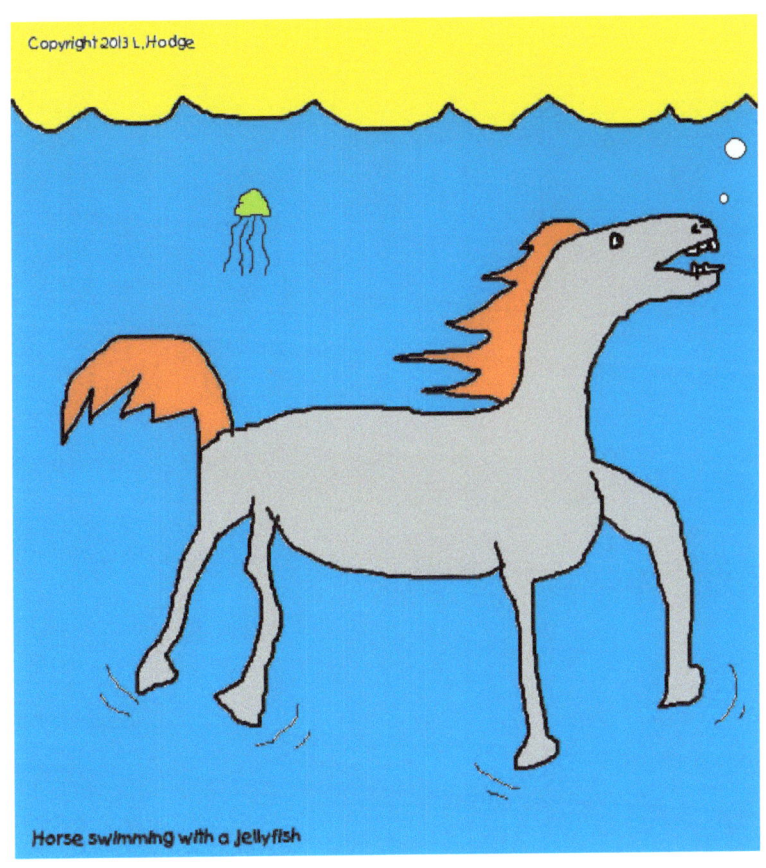

Horse swimming with a jellyfish

33

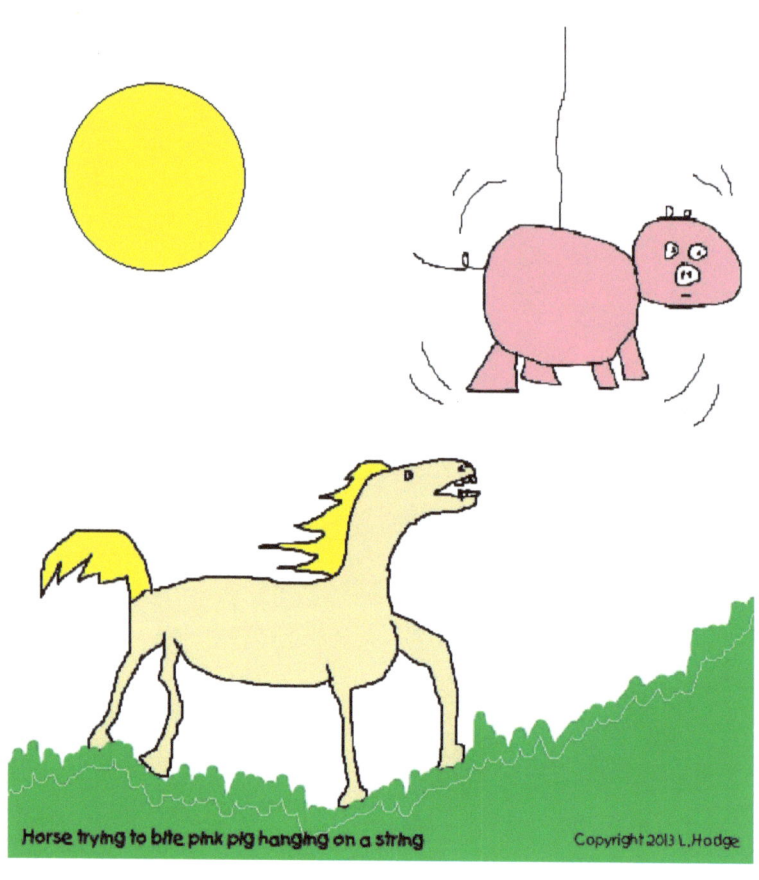

Horse trying to bite pink pig hanging on a string

Copyright 2013 L. Hodge

Horse trying to bite pink pig hanging on a string

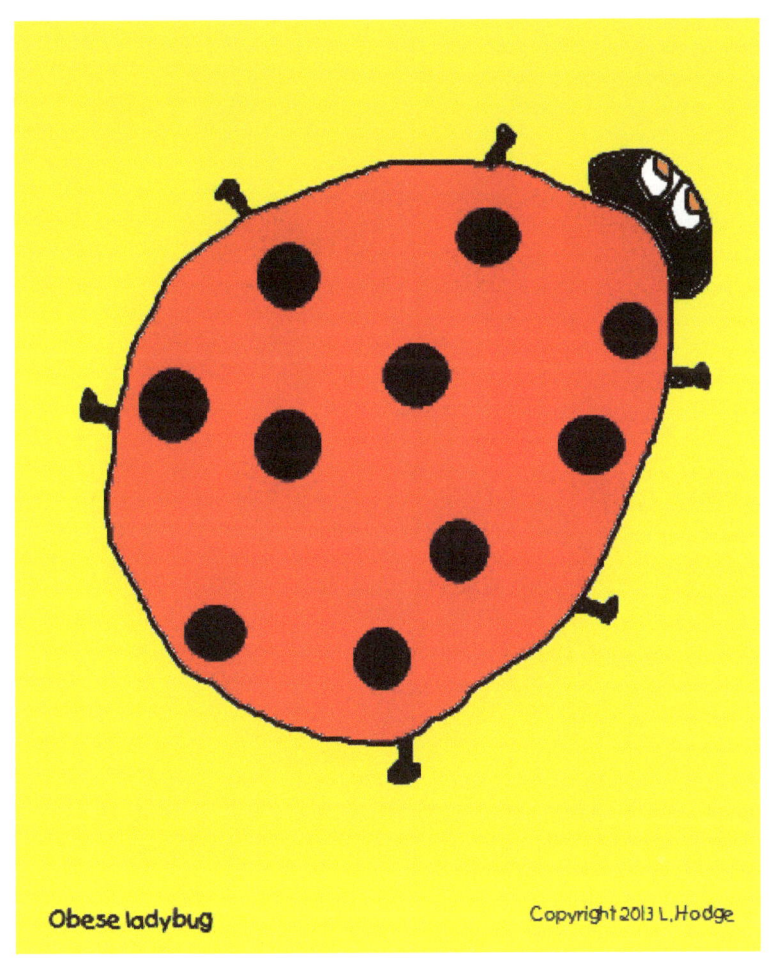

Obese ladybug

Obese ladybug

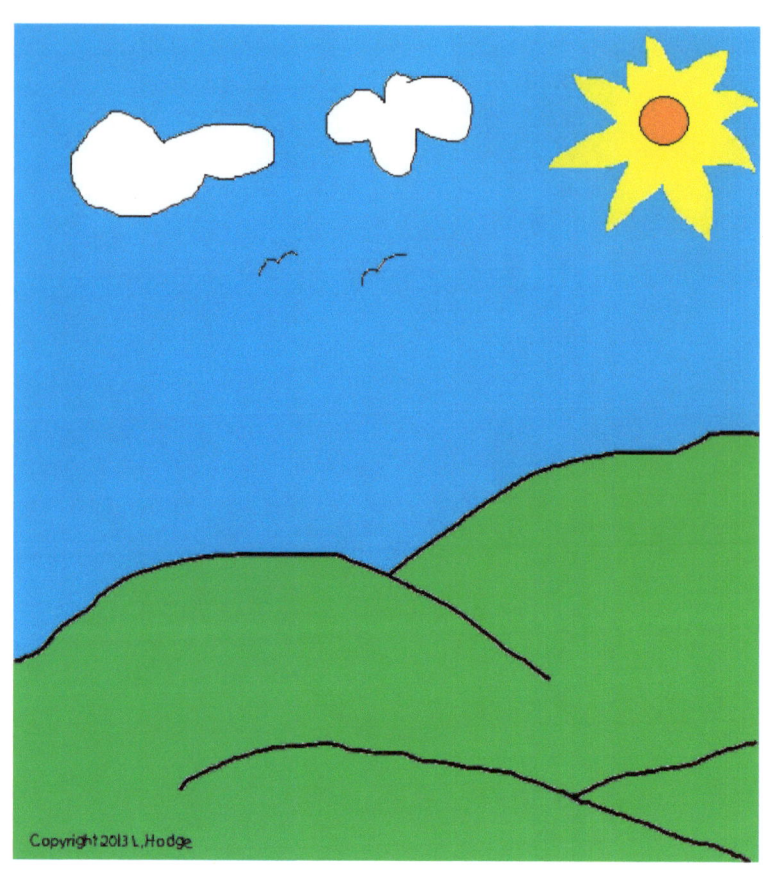

Copyright 2013 L, Hodge

Landscape and birds

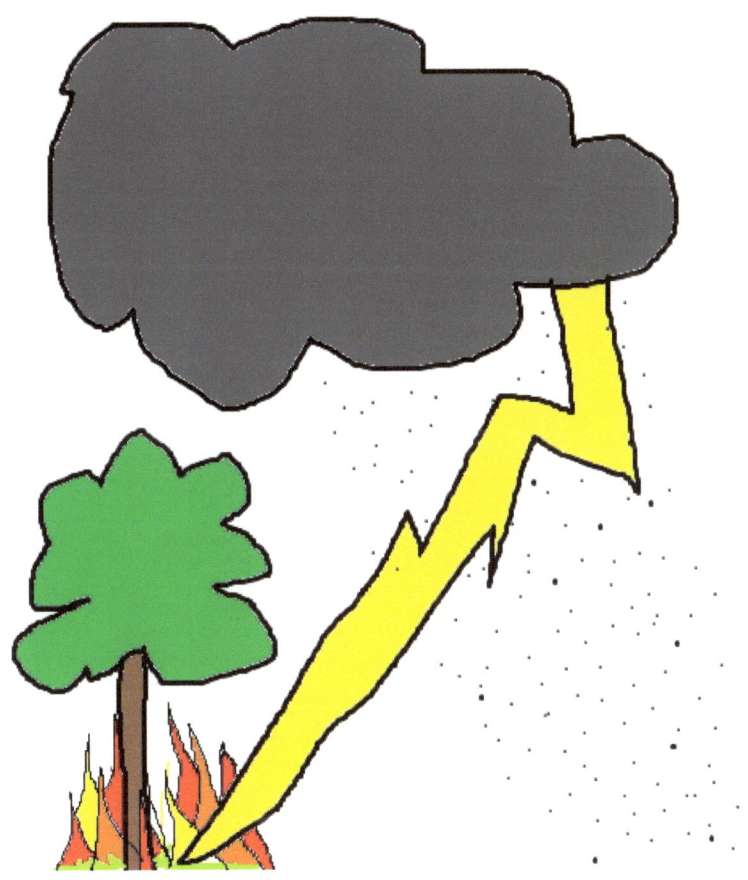

Ironic

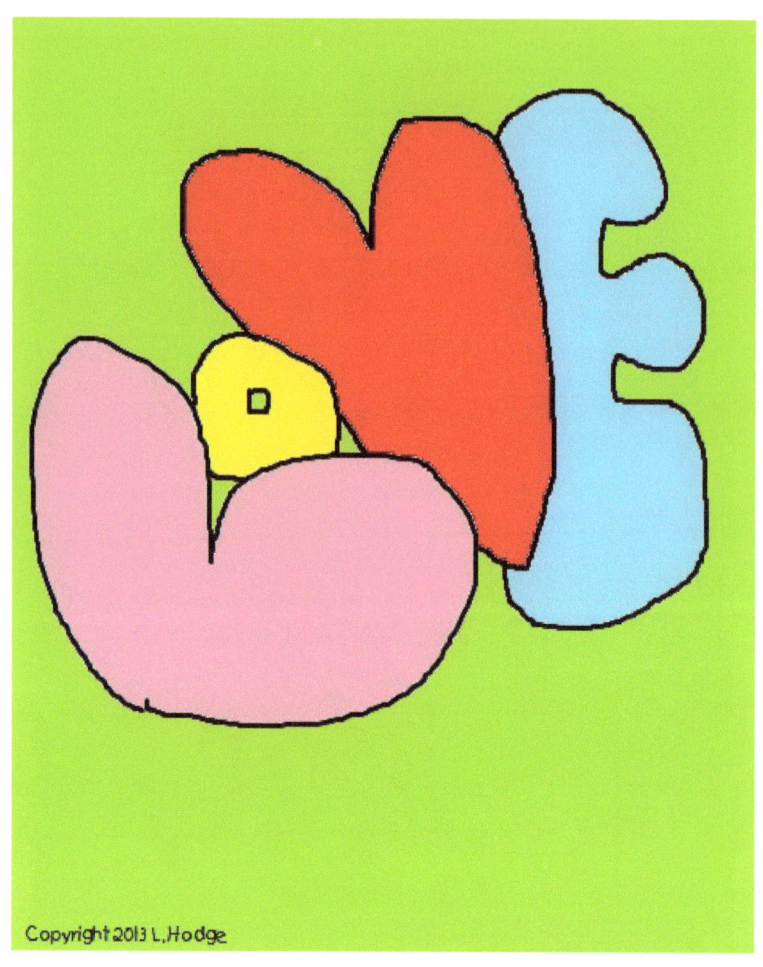

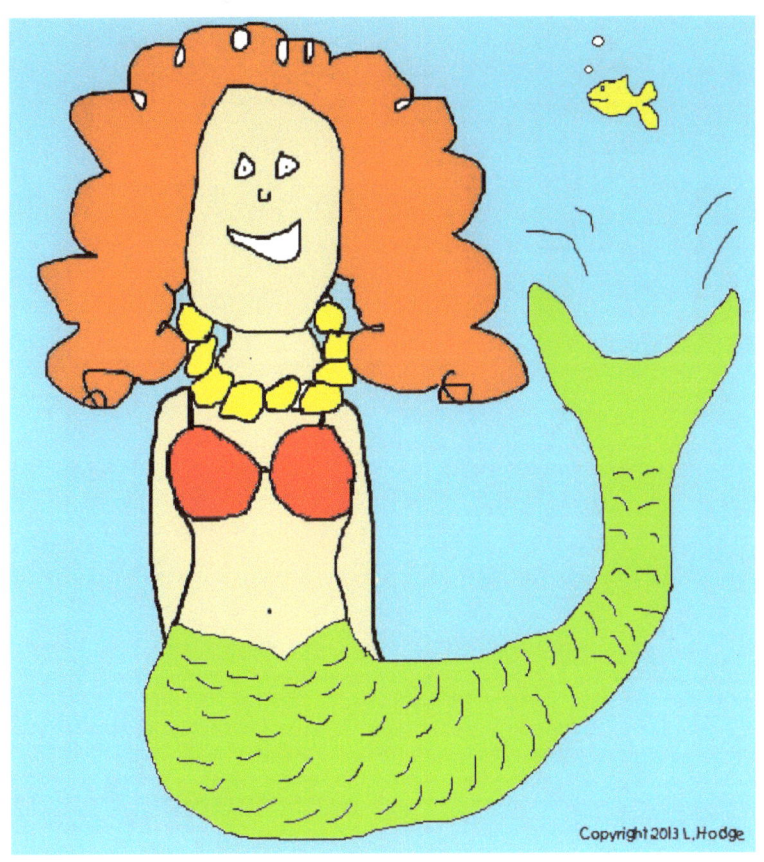

Girl with no legs

Period 2
Mr. Marron / Creative writing

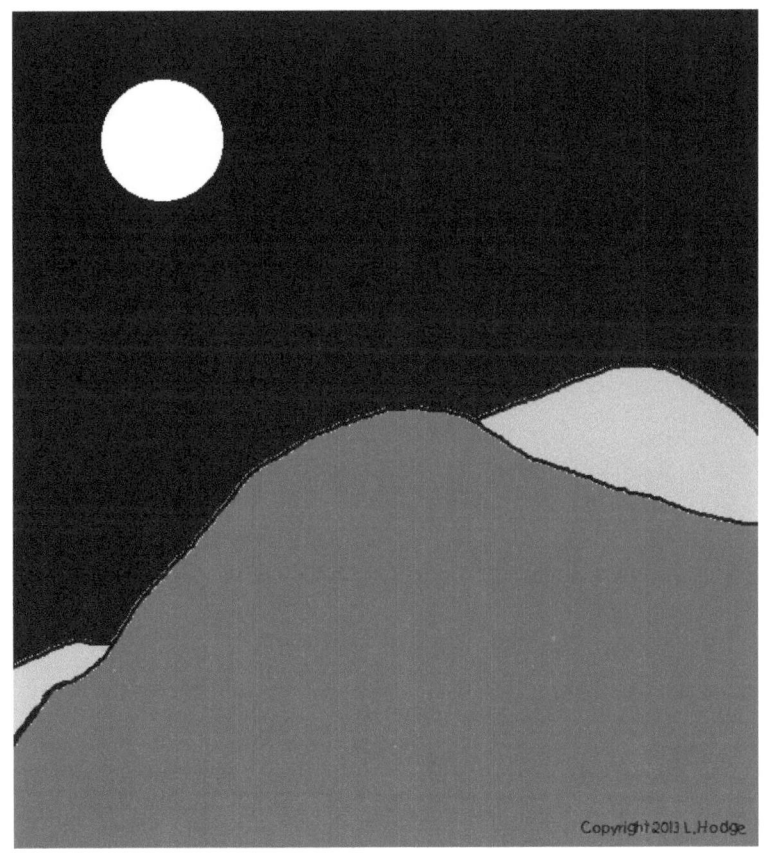

Night

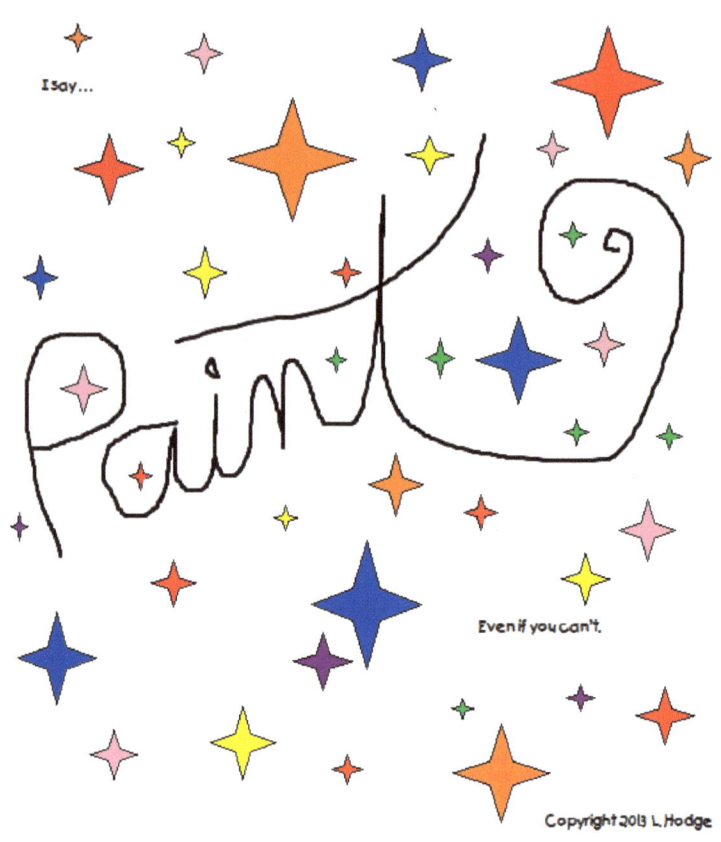

I say...

Even if you can't.

42

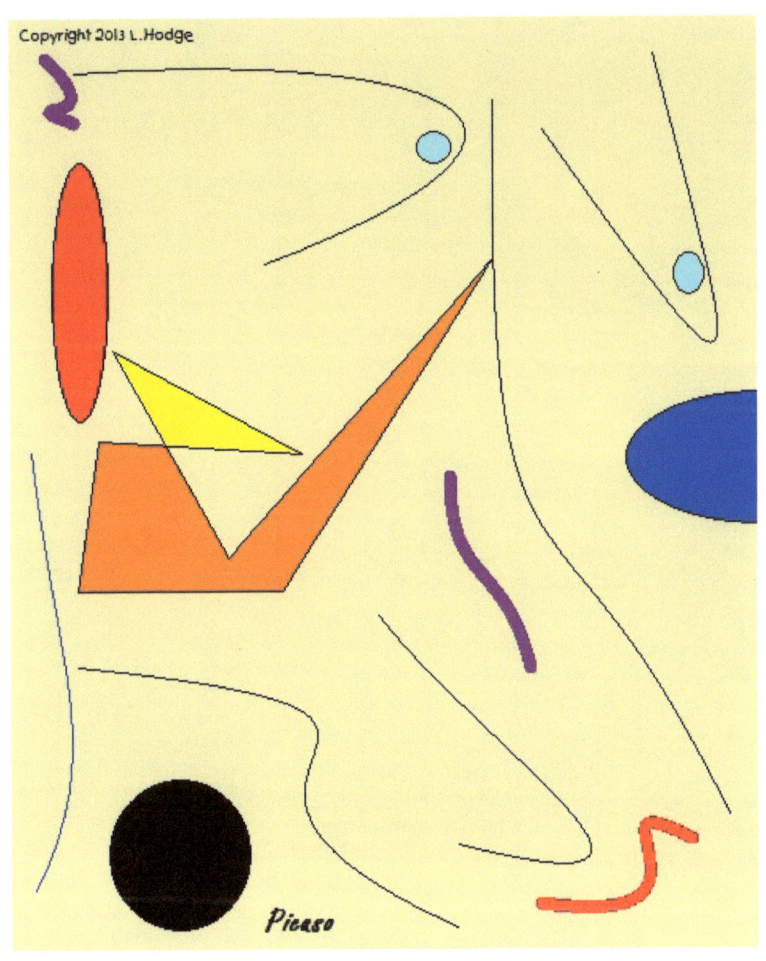

Picasso with one 's'

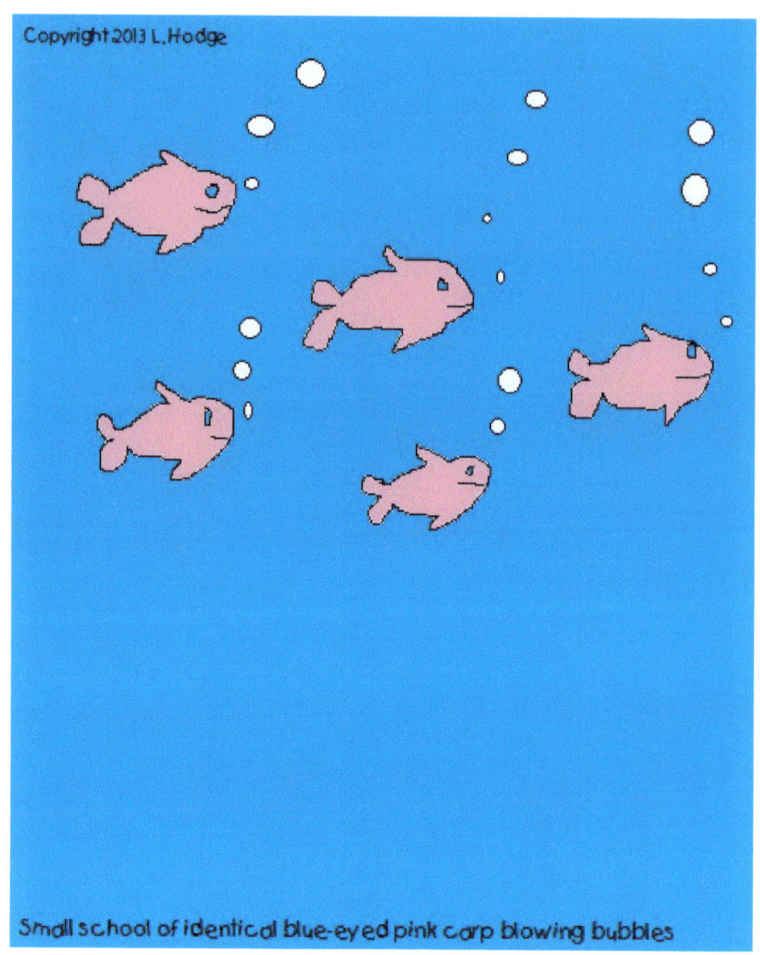

Small school of identical blue-eyed pink carp blowing bubbles

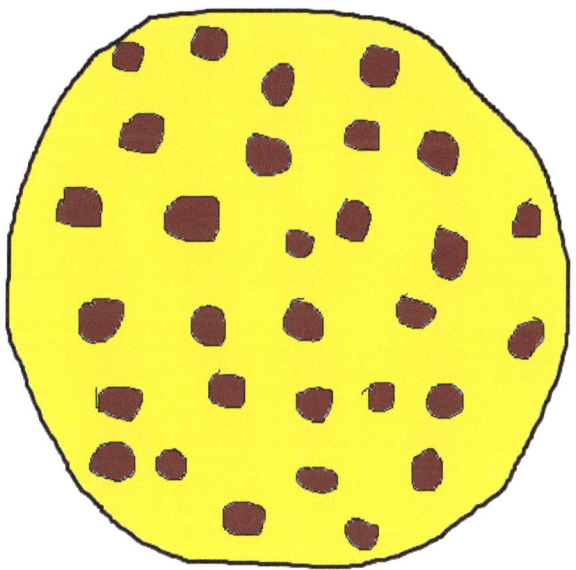

Pepperoni with cheese hold the sauce

Period 2
Mr. Marron / Creative writing

The hills seemed to glow with the promise of today
Yesterday faded away with each new breeze
And a bluejay shouted out 'Today, today!'
This is the stuff of memories, sweet hot memories
Of another summer, another morning, another
chance.

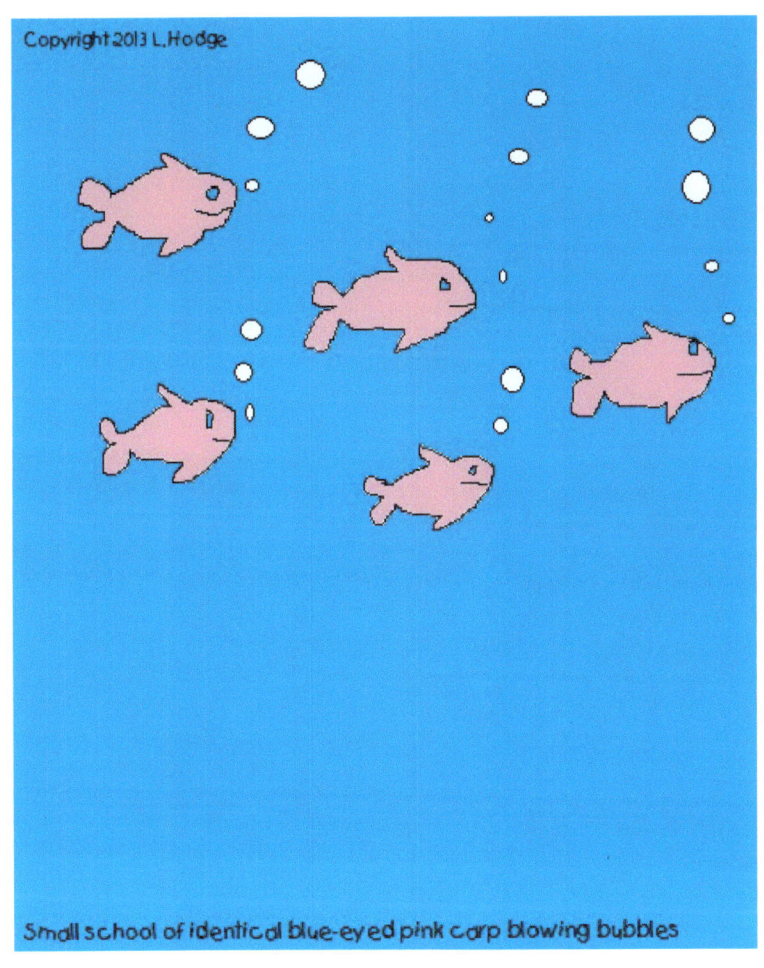

Small school of identical blue-eyed pink carp blowing bubbles

Fish from page 44 coming through

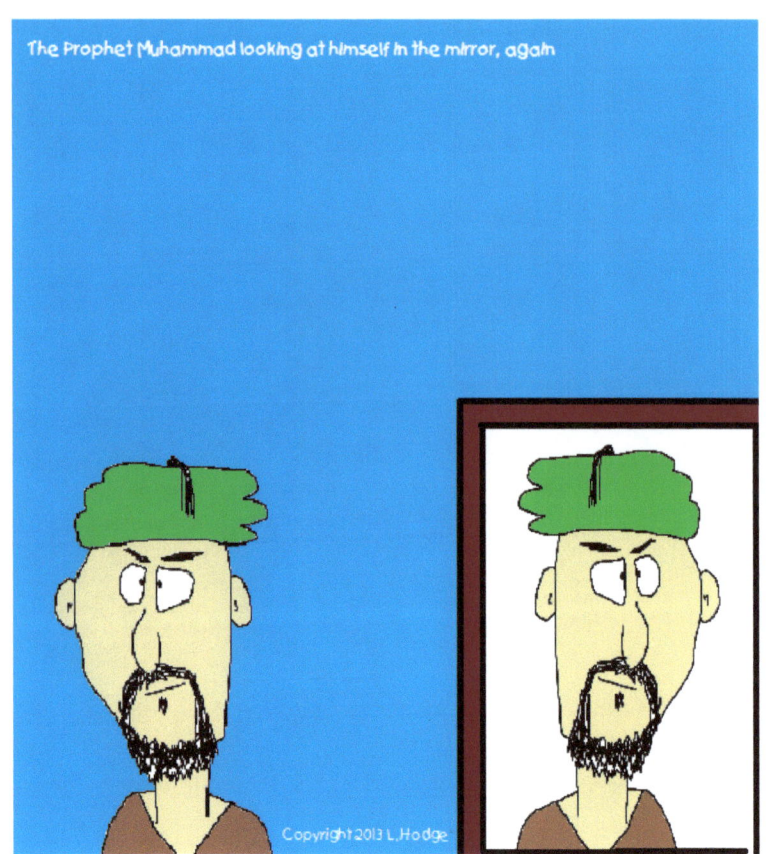

The Prophet Muhammad looking at himself in the mirror, again

Copyright 2013 L. Hodge

So this is your new puppy? Humm. His back legs are sort of pointy. What's up with his ears, they're different sizes? Why does his tongue hang out like that? He's got a weird body. No, I like him, he's cute, what's his name? Oh, well you should give him a name. No I don't want him, I have a dog. Really? Then why did you say he's your new puppy? What's wrong with you? You did what? Bath salts? I've never heard of that. That sounds dangerous. No, I don't do that. Ok, but just a little. Wow. This is dangerous. What? Oh, I thought you said something. Let's call him Dr. Drew... (laughing). Yeah... he's cool. His tongue is cool. I wish my dog had pointy legs. Come here Drew! He's stupid (laughing). That's a nice puppy. I want him (laughing)

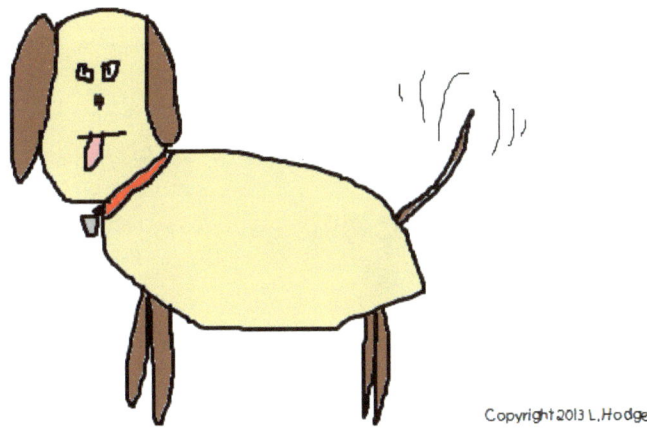

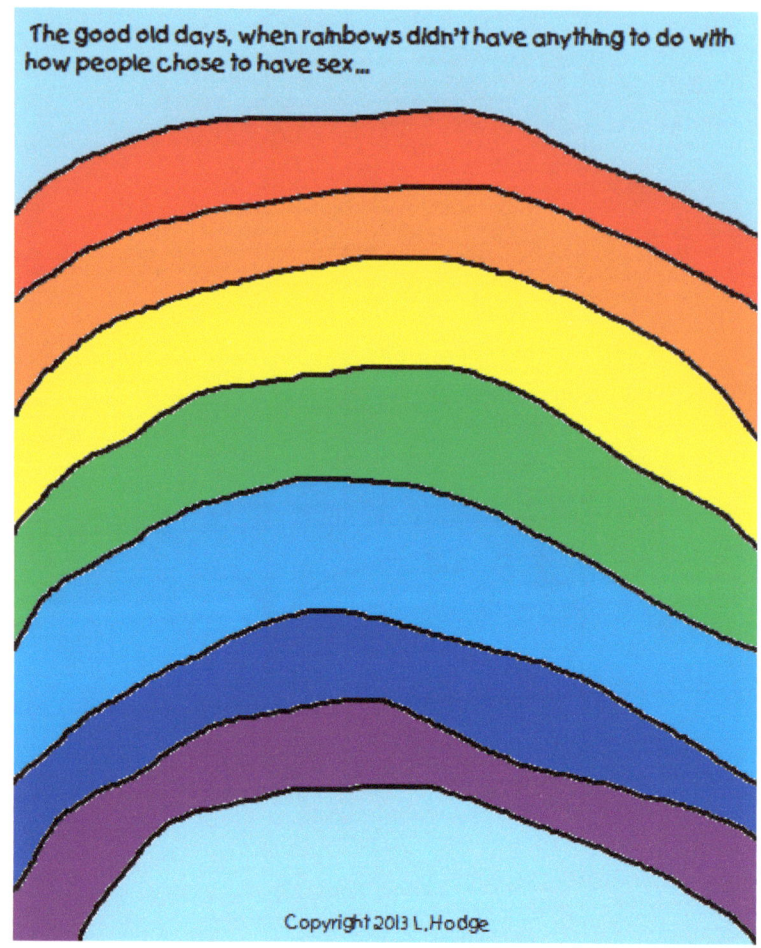

The good old days, when rainbows didn't have anything to do with how people chose to have sex...

Copyright 2013 L. Hodge

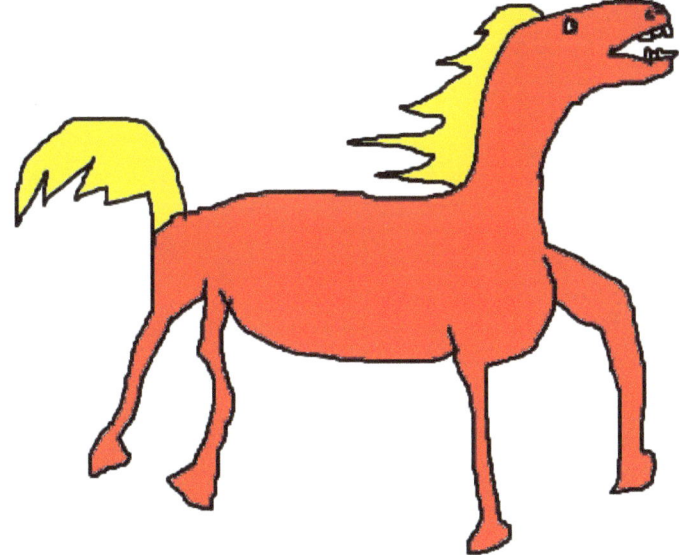

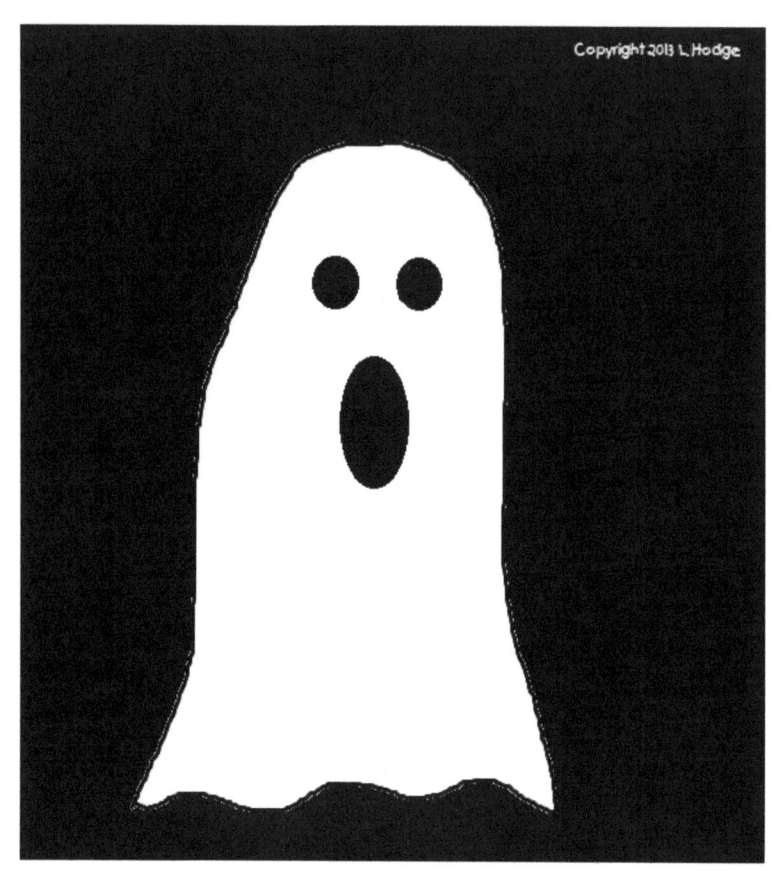

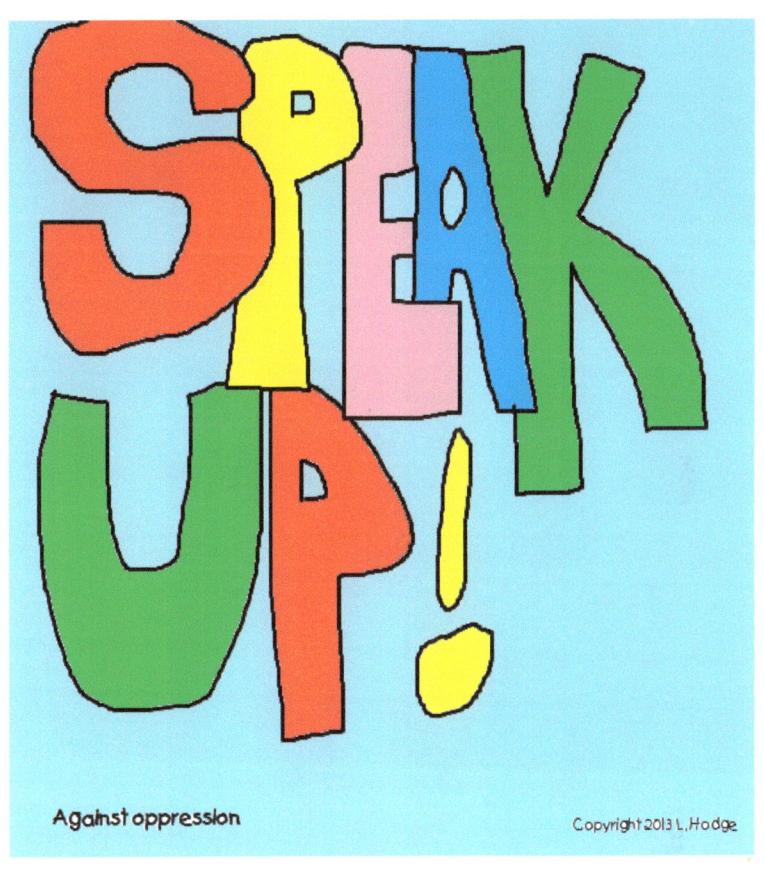

Against oppression

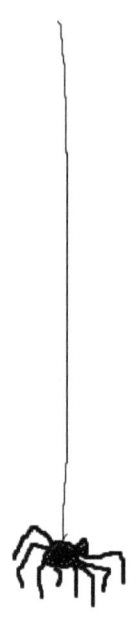

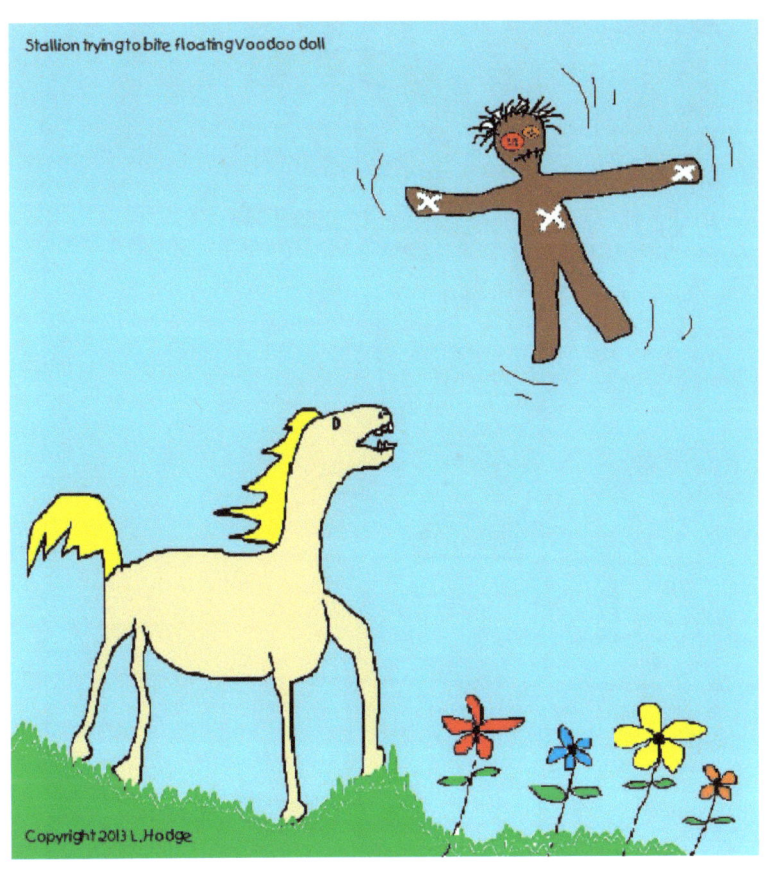

Stallion trying to bite floating Voodoo doll

Copyright 2013 L. Hodge

Stallion trying to bite floating Voodoo doll

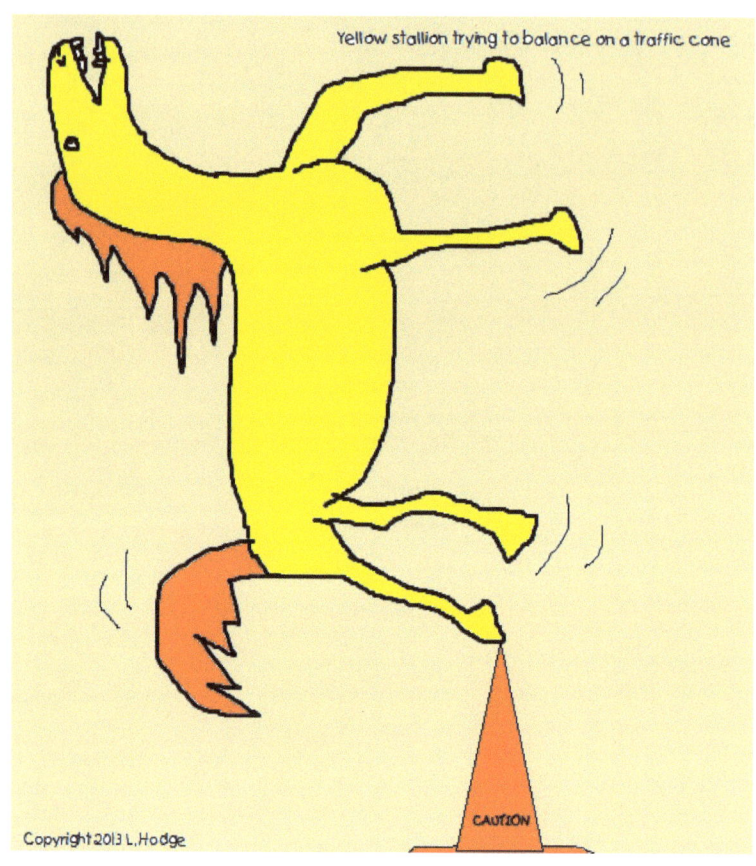

Yellow stallion trying to
balance on a traffic cone

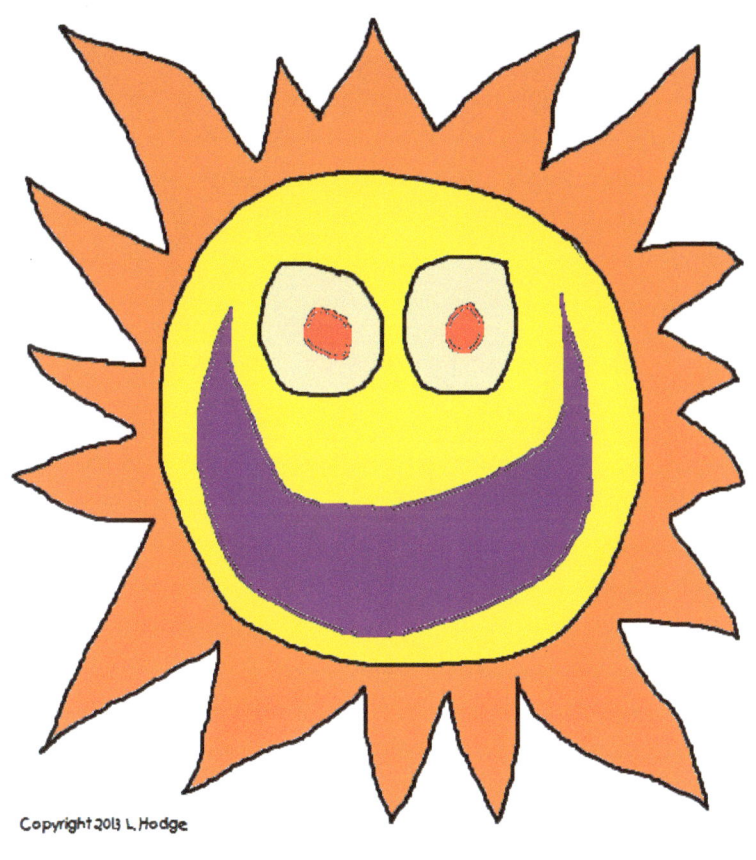

Sun with purple smile

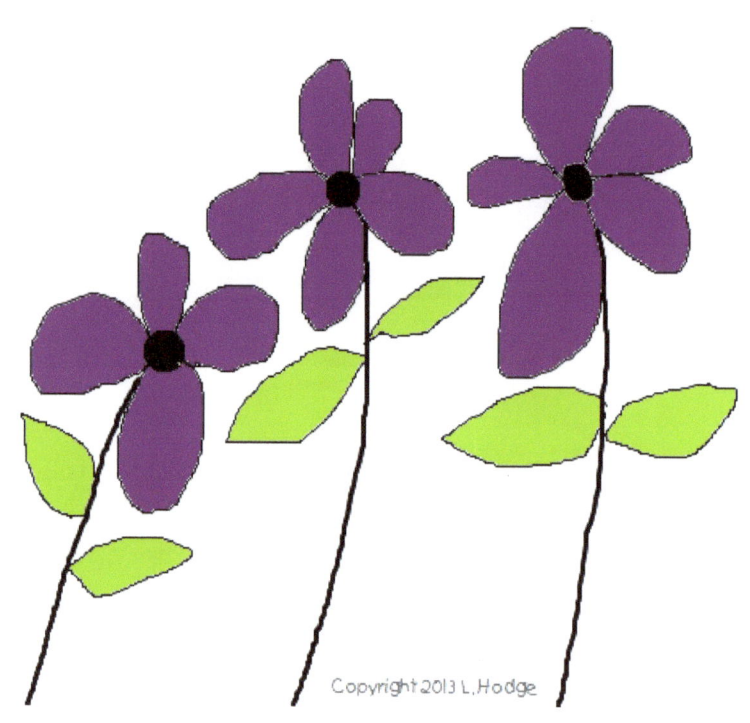

Copyright 2013 L. Hodge

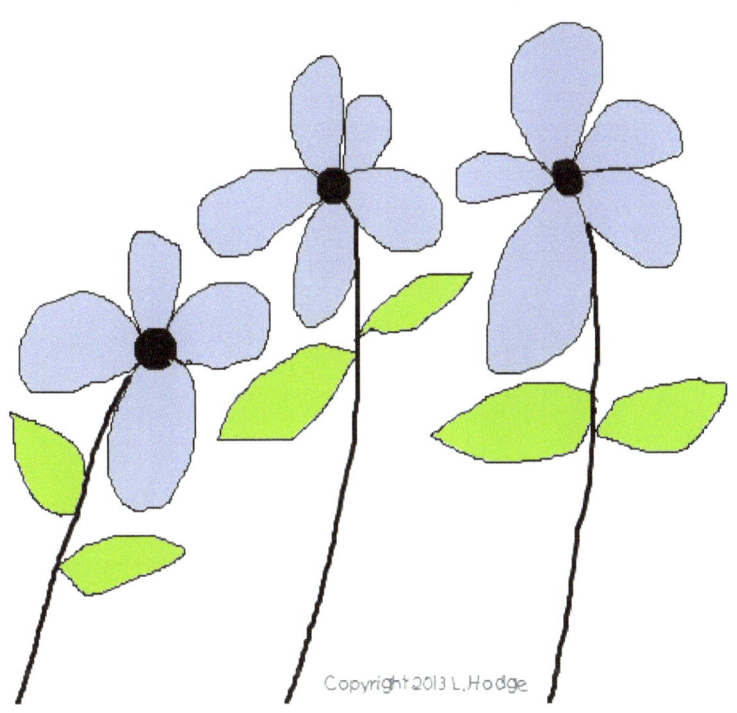

Copyright 2013 L. Hodge

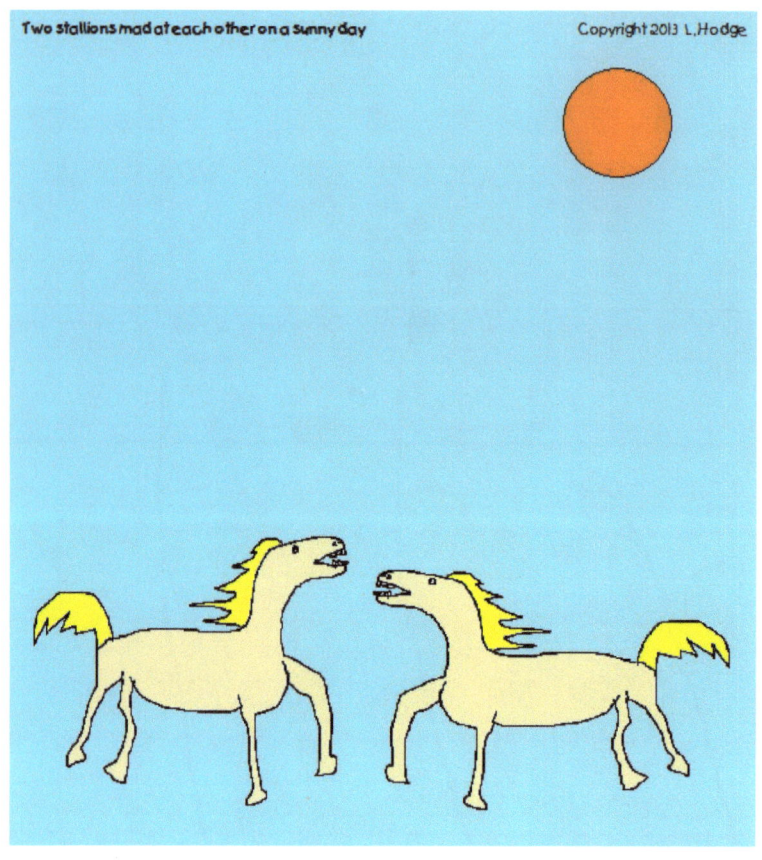

Two stallions mad at each other
on a sunny day

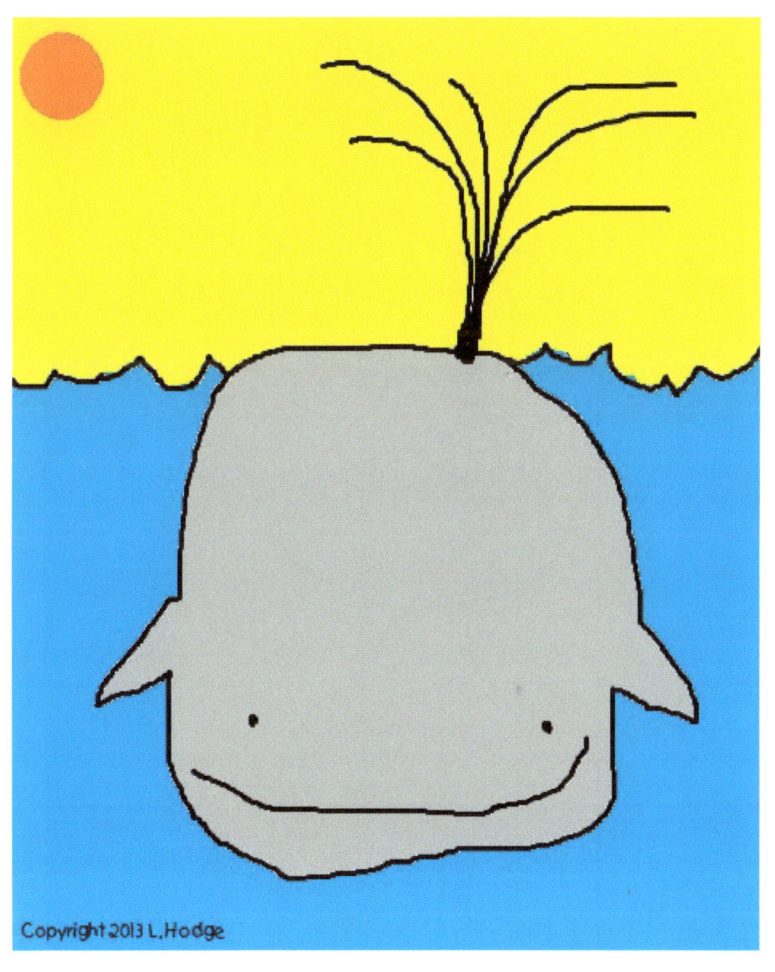

Copyright 2013 L. Hodge

Whale looking right at you

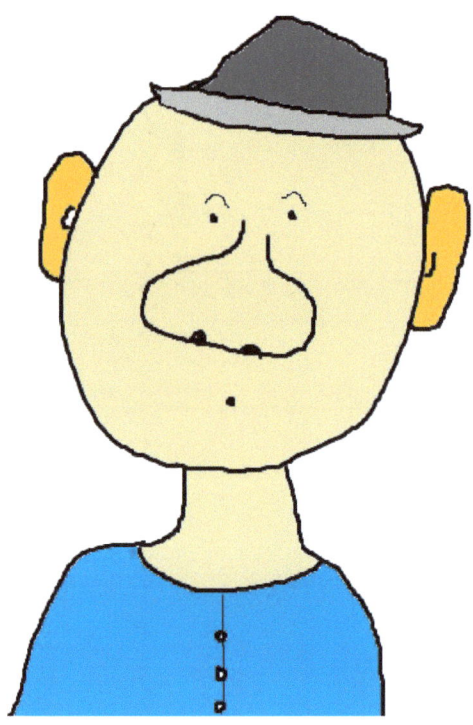

The Whistler

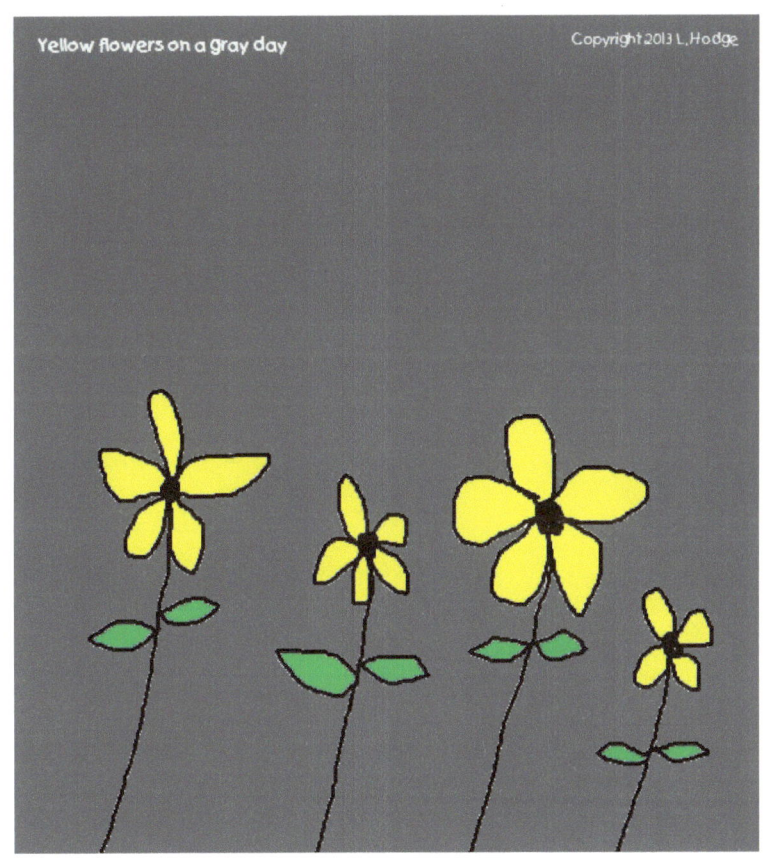

Yellow flowers on a gray day

Yellow flowers on a gray day

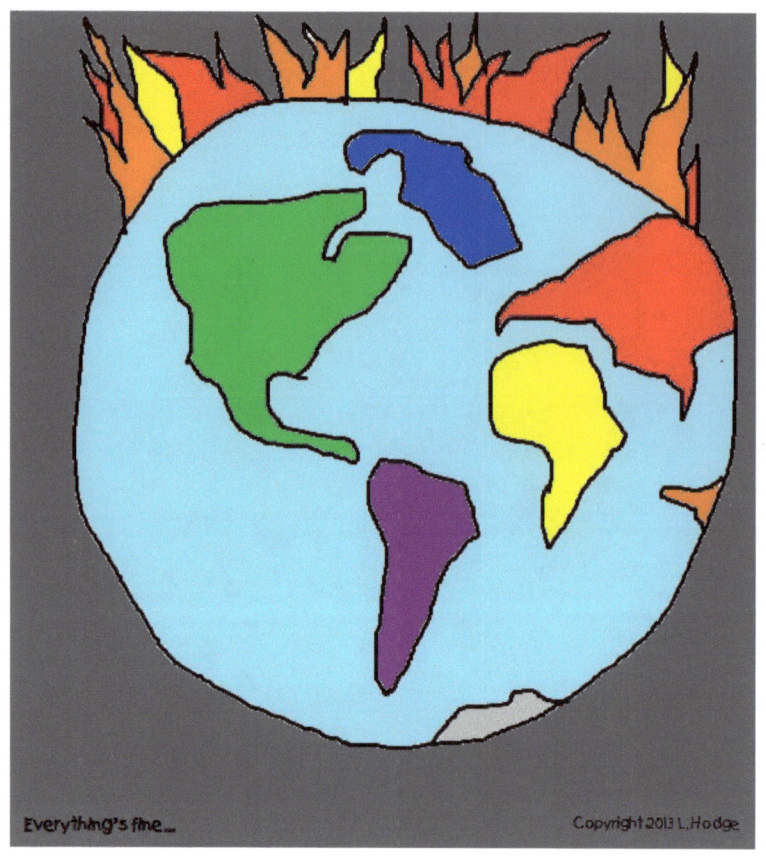

Everything's fine...

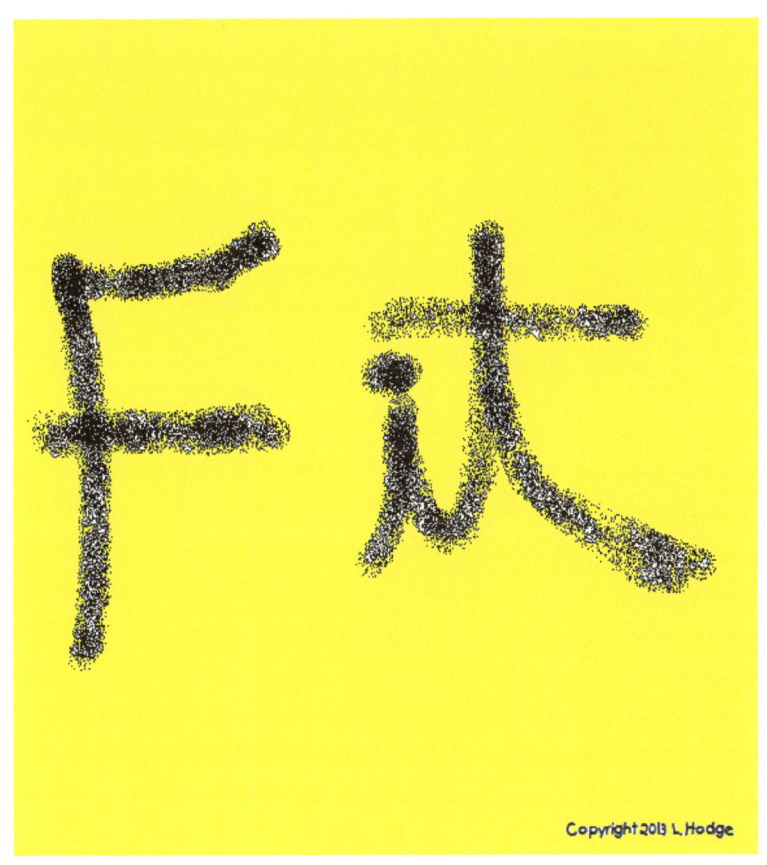

Copyright 2013 L. Hodge

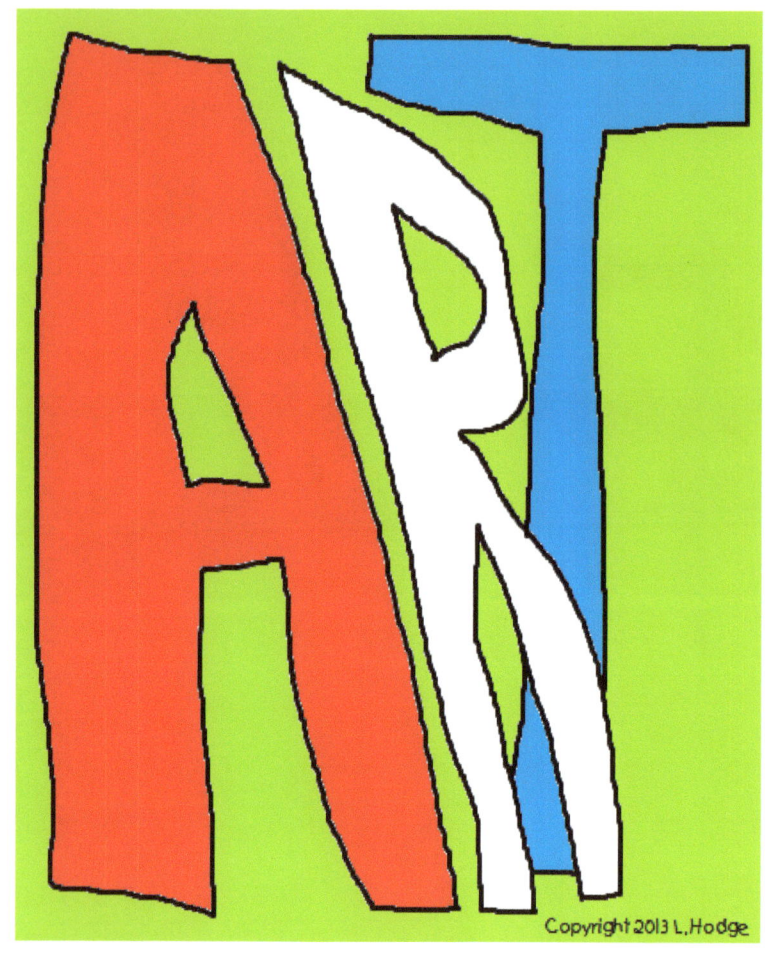

Copyright 2013 L. Hodge

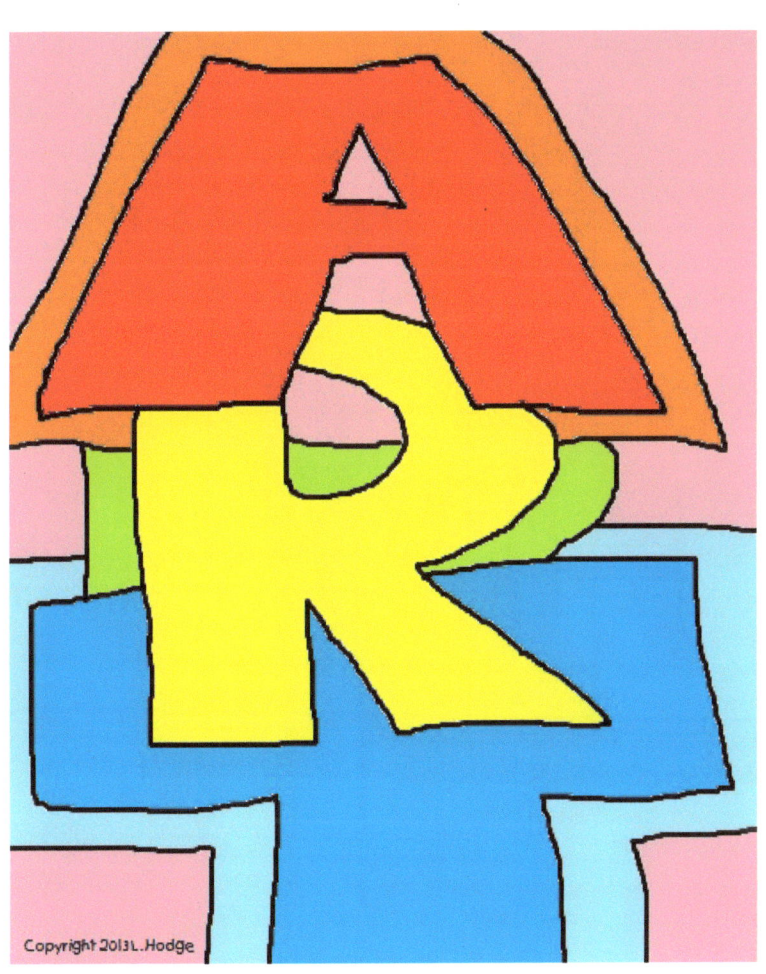

Copyright 2013 L. Hodge

67

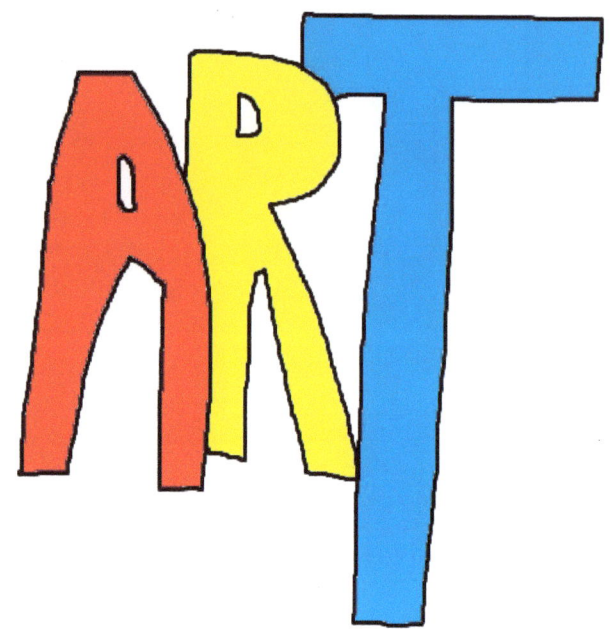

Copyright 2013 L. Hodge

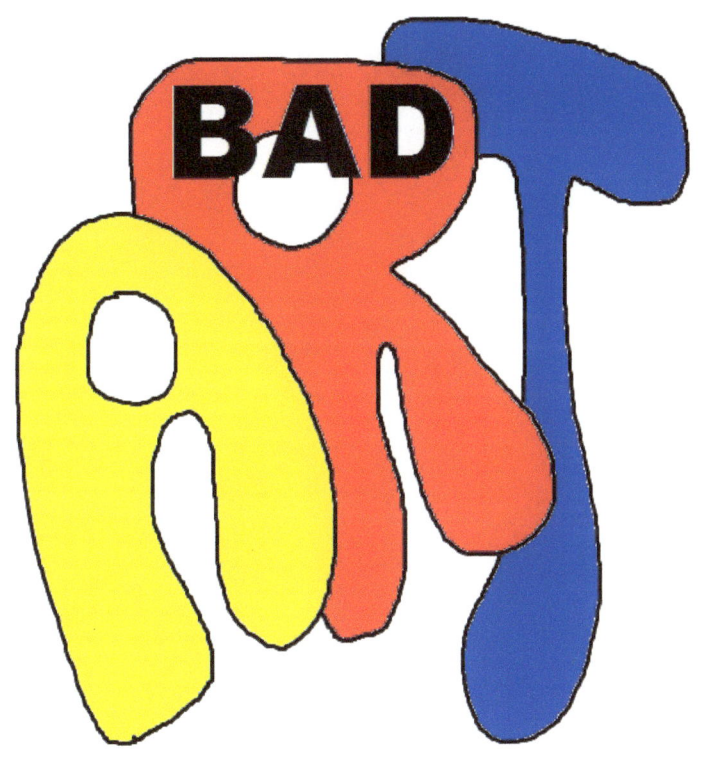

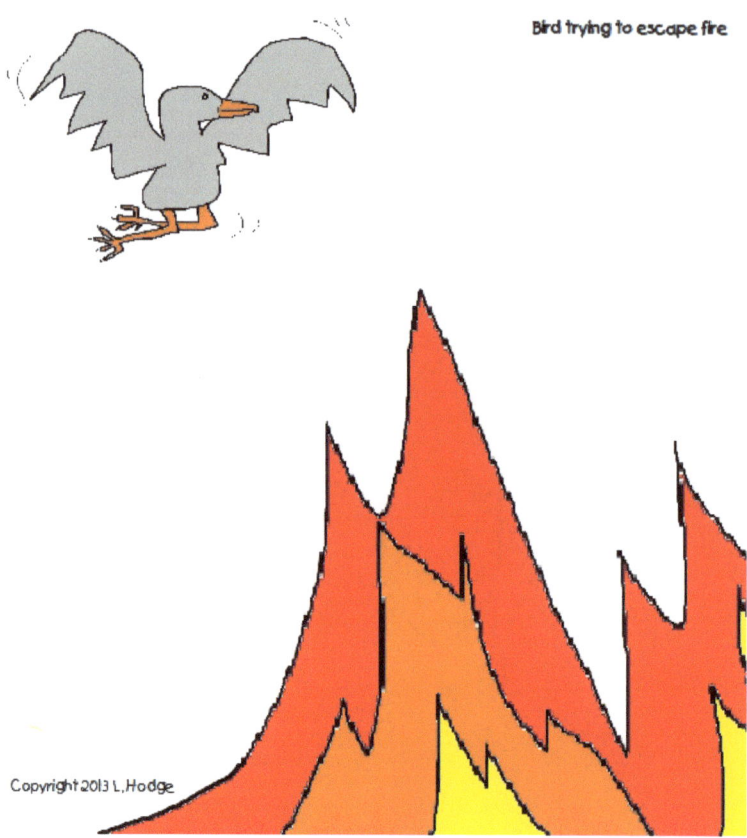

Bird trying to escape fire

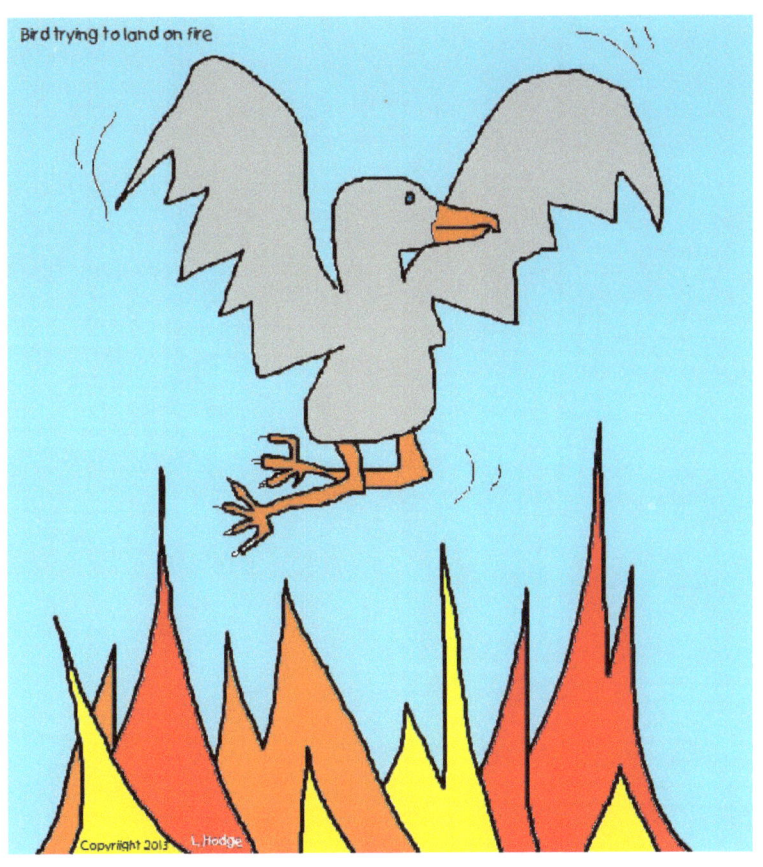

Bird trying to land on fire

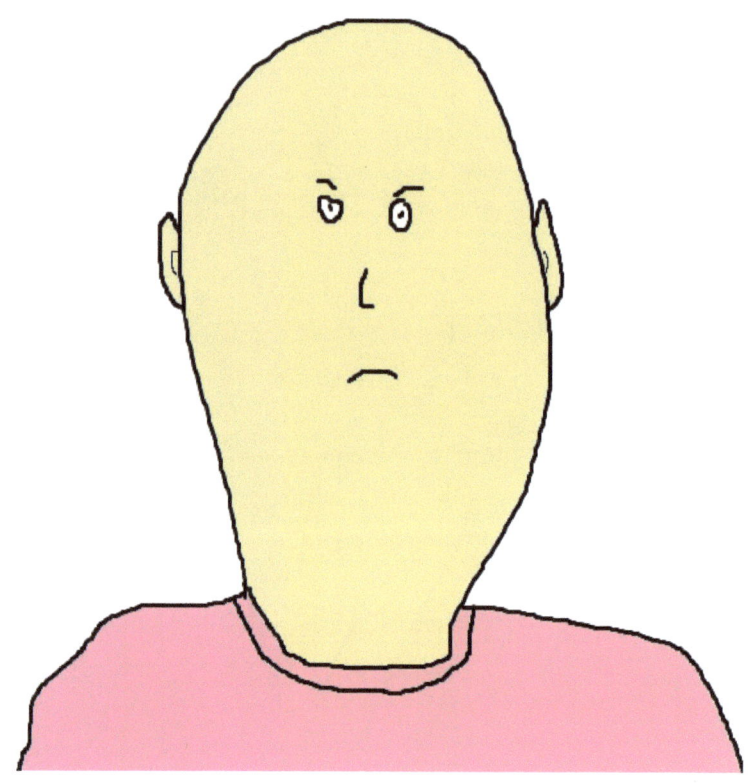

Man unhappy with birthday gift

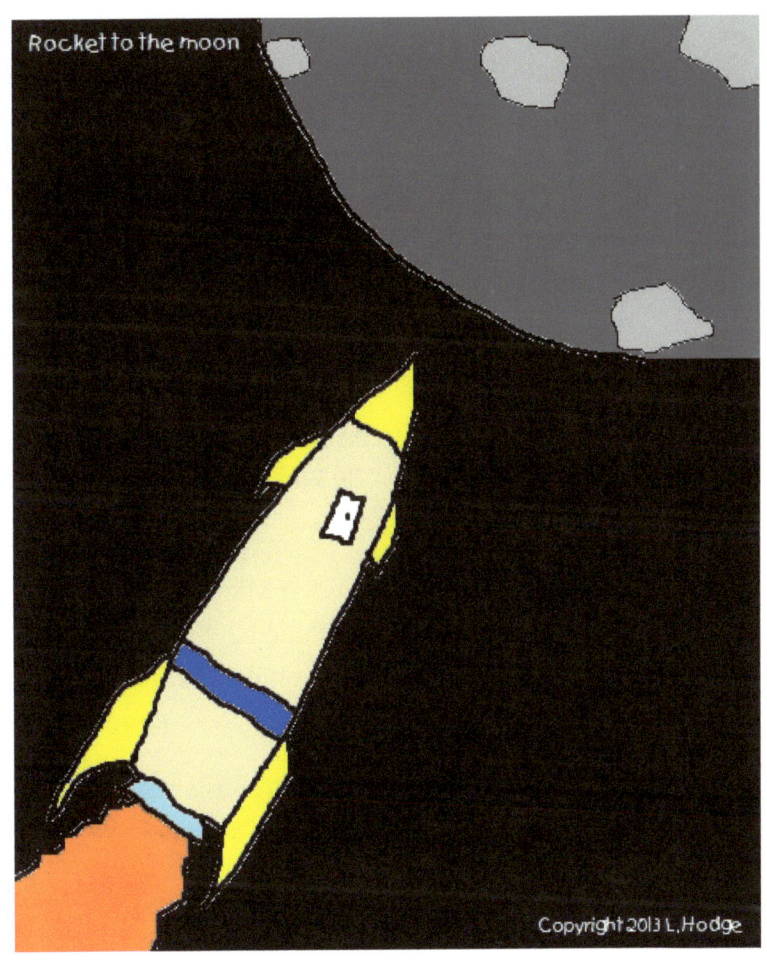

Rocket to the moon

Copyright 2013 L. Hodge

Art from book one here again in book two

Epilogue

Well, well, well. I hope you enjoyed that journey. I know I did, especially the rocket at the end, and the school of fish that swam through on pages 44 and 47.

I could go on and on about my favorite moments, how about Page 48, well, to any Muslim assassins I would just like to say that I had nothing to do with *that* picture, the editor did that (Marion Spencer, 126 Elm Grove, Las Vegas, Nevada). Please take up any grievances with her.

For those of you who look for 'Hidden Mickeys' or 'clues' in books and amusement parks; on Page 62, "The Whistler", you probably figured it out but he is whistling a "Bb."

And, on Page 60, those Stallions, they weren't really mad at each other, you can see them smiling if you look close.

Page 54, yes, there were *eight* legs on that spider.

Page 51, yes, there are *real* horses that color, they are called "Arabian Sparklers."

Page 33, "Horse swimming with jellyfish" was inspired by a *YouTube* video of an actual horse swimming in the ocean. I added the jellyfish part.

Page 4, "Blue Stallion", yes, there are *real* horses *that* color, they are called "Blueberry Palominos."

Pages 7 and 9 speak for themselves, and the girl on Page 12, that was *Candice Ann Collins*, a girl I loved in the sixth grade. She was even prettier than that.

Page 31, well, maybe flowers don't have such thoughts, but maybe they do, I'd rather like to think they do.

And finally, Page 28, "Camel in the sun", ah, the look in his eye, the expression on his mouth, he's so proud of how nice his humps look today, just *perfect*.

I hope the above insight into the creation of this artwork helped you to better understand it, and art in general. Next time you look at a work of art stop and think for a moment about what the *art* is thinking. But don't do that for very long, it's only an exercise, a ridiculous one to see how long you would think about how inanimate art can think, which should be about *one* second, and then you realize it's a stupid exercise since art *doesn't* think, but artists do, sometimes, but that's not so important, just look at the art, then figure out where you're going for lunch.

Please cherish this book and share it with your friends, but don't let them keep it, they might spill something on it, maybe buy them one and let them spill on their own copy.

It's a good bet that there won't be a *third* book in the series, two books like this is *plenty*. Of course they'll be more art, an artist *must* draw, but I'll keep that art to myself, I'll hang it on my own walls and stare at it until I'm sick of it and then I'll burn it.

Speaking of burning. On Page 64, if you thought the *Earth* was on fire in that drawing, it wasn't. You can tell by the continents it isn't Earth, it's *Kolob,* and the Mormons are going to be pissed when they find out it has flames at its North Pole. Although it *is* an accurate rendering of the planet Kolob, the artwork itself *was* meant to be symbolic, and yes, of *Earth.* You know, 'Everything's fine...' and you wonder what comes after the ...

...well, that's the beauty of art, the *appreciation* of it, the *worth* of it, and the *meaning* of it, some would say 'art' is in the eye of the beholder, but that saying is really meant for *beauty,* so let's just say "ART", well, that's really what *you* decide, you are the judge of what is art and what is just some wanna-be artist's feeble attempt at art. But think for a moment what Michelangelo, or Renoir, or Leonardo de Vinci, Monet, Matisse, Rembrandt, Rubens, Degas, Dali (not the Lama), Raphael, Cezanne, Chagall, or even Picasso, what all their first attempts and early works must have looked like, most likely much like the *Master Work* you just viewed on Page 34, *that* piece was a recreation of an early Rembrandt that hangs today in the Louvre (yes the French do spell funny).

So there we go, some art, some history, some perspective, some facts, some fiction, but that's life isn't it? Mostly fiction with a few facts mixed in to keep you wondering? Well it is. I've come to the end of this book and yet it feels somehow incomplete, perhaps, as I mentioned earlier, we've looked at the art, and now, it's time to figure out where you're going for lunch.

Cela fait beaucoup, je l' avoue.

Lance Hodge

www.ingramcontent.com/pod-product-compliance
Lightning Source LLC
Chambersburg PA
CBHW040833180526
45159CB00001B/176